CONTENTS

CONTENTS

HEALTH AND SOCIAL SERVICES:
Collaboration or Conflict?

John Chant *et al.*

Discussion Paper No. 14

Policy Studies Institute

Sales Representation: Frances Pinter (Publishers) Ltd.

Orders to: Marston Book Services, P.O. Box 87, Oxford OX4 1LB

ISBN 0-85374-310 X

Published by Policy Studies Institute
100 Park Village East, London NW1 3SR
Printed by Bourne Offset Ltd.

FOREWORD

Tim Nodder
Former Deputy Secretary responsible for Services Development, Department of Health and Social Security.

Joint planning for health and social services is not a topic that arouses instant enthusiasm. Most of the attenders at a day conference on the subject are likely to be quite heavily involved already. The same will no doubt be true of most readers of these papers.

Social insects - ants, for example - are able to co-ordinate the activities of their complex communities by instinctively releasing and detecting subtle chemical combinations. We, being human, have to work at these problems. This requires of us two things: on the one hand, to maintain interest, attention and motivation; on the other, to identify and establish skills.

A day seminar such as the one at the Policy Studies Institute in London on 28 June 1985, under the joint auspices of the Association of Directors of Social Services and the Institute, is an opportunity to rekindle enthusiasm. The subsequent perusal of the papers presented ought to reinforce this, and remind us of practical points to be followed up.

The immediate perspective is now right. For two years and more the NHS has been an enfeebled partner in collaborative local efforts because of the unhinging effects of its severe managerial changes. But this must no longer afford excuses. The Report of the Select Committee for Social Services on Community Care, (Second Report from the Social Services Committee, Session 1984-85), and the publication of the Government's response (Cmnd 9674)

1

at dates which straddled this conference, have pointed up large fields for which joint planning and operations are essential. Other current DHSS initiatives, such as the support of the self-help movement and the combatting of drug misuse, also call for skills and confidence in matching up the contributions of the non-statutory sectors. Many separate agencies are also combining to develop services to handle alcohol abuse, the field in which I am working at present.

Historical perspective
In beginning this section with a reminiscence of the campaign against Malayan insurgents, I underline the age of my evidence. Interesting accounts became available around 1960 of how the British commanders used painstakingly compiled profiles of each affected district to help them determine the tactical planning for their 'hearts and minds' operations. I envisaged something of the sort as a tool-kit for the health planners of the health service we were then proposing - for the first time - to unify. (In December 1985, Mr Miles Hardie, Director-General of the International Hospital Federation, wrote to The Times to inspire us with a similar account of patch and map tactics used today in health development in Costa Rica!) Coupled with these notions were ideas drawn from themes of business management, the principal point being the importance of the 'accountable unit' or (in commercial terms) profit centre. Laid alongside were the truly shocking research accounts of failures between the general practitioner and hospital services to communicate either on the level of the individual patient or on operational policies.

While these notions were fermenting in the background, the foreground was occupied by the catalytic first Hospital Plan. This Plan had been driven along by Mr Enoch Powell's enthusiasm, with Mr Gedling stoking in the Ministry of Health, as it then was, boiler room. The short sequence of local authority social services Ten Year Plans followed as a proper complement, though there was apparent a certain threadbareness of exchanges between the various local and regional levels.

Fresh with Treasury experience of the introduction of forward costings in the defence budget, I took to heart the possibilities opened up by the NHS/Social Services forward looks. The central 'George Brown' White Papers on the progress of the economy made it reasonable to adopt a long-term planning view that was avowedly expansionist. There would be room for change. The incremental readings of the spending figures and overseas evidence of 'higher wealth, more spending on health' seemed convincing. This was a time for planning enthusiasm. But the flame went down. Building costs soaring above estimates, site problems, size problems - all the dangers of a capital-led planning style became apparent. Rarely were the local authority services au courant with the increasingly cautious and hidden agendas of the hospital authorities.

The spring tide of the Ten Year Plans left its high water debris on the bookshelves of Whitehall and receded.

Happily a second exciting phase of joint planning flowed in more naturally behind the break-up of the tripartite NHS and the first unifying reorganisation. At this time the local government health facilities were brought alongside the hospital services. The fortunate Scots brought in the general practitioner services as well.

In England, we sought to cash in our notions of compact territorial units of accountability. We saw it as important that there should be service to a common population by a health authority and a strengthened social care department. What a pity that this positive concept, aimed at people and their needs, has been so battered!

First, by contested reforms that drew and redrew the map of local government.

Second, by the battle over 'co-terminosity' of health and local social care units - a battle that was eventually lost, so far as I was concerned. Perhaps the mistake was to accept the very term, since 'co-terminosity' emphasises the boundaries, whereas our original hopes were that the services would be about people within areas and their needs.

Third, the hospital interests, coming late to grips with their own discovery of the ideal 'district general hospital' could not be persuaded to raise their viewpoint, at that time, to the wider ideal of community area provision.

None the less, the models of area needs and service planning became more familiar as the reorganisation worked through. These models became a staple of the enhanced management training of the 1970s. We began to see the first fruits of a cadre of staff at regional and other levels who were accustomed to work with planning vocabularies that were much richer than the capital-framed planning documents of the 1960s.

There was an aberrant period after 1979 when some of these skills were driven underground by the rhetoric of 'all back to the districts'. It was ideologically unsound to consider any resurrection of forward looks within local/central government exchanges. However, the afficionados of the planning tables persisted with their guidelines and their SASPs (Summary Analysis of Strategic Plans).

The pressures of economic realism that had battered away the original ten year plans forced the adoption of good housekeeping on the macro scale as well as in minutiae. Regional NHS reviews now provide the field on which planners' skills confront political imperatives.

The Seminar
Thus, with memories and myths of past moments of enthusiasm, I approached the Policy Studies Institute, and now recall the discussion and re-read the papers.

In its response to the Select Committee on Community Care, published in November 1985, the Government confirmed its commitment to the development of the network of central policies and local services necessary for community care. It said it would continue to impress on statutory authorities their responsibilities for joint planning. Good practice it will encourage (para. 6). I am glad to read that General Managers have been reminded of the 'development of local solutions to local problems in the light of local resources and informed by consultation, consumer research, and regular contact with voluntary bodies' (para. 10). By their actions we shall judge them!

The Joint Planning Working Group initiated by the National Association of Health Authorities and the Local Authority Associations also reported last year. This report has been published as Progress in Partnership, but at the time I write no decisive advice has been issued based upon it. There will presumably be endorsement of its main points: the need for links at both member and officer level, and for liaison in drawing up plans and not just in looking at them. Another key point is that there should be joint planning of total service resource use, not merely joint finance.

Recommendations are spelt out for designating senior managers with responsibilities for promoting joint planning, for posts of joint planning co-ordinator, and for project co-ordinators 'sufficiently senior to wield the necessary authority'. This emphasis on persons rather than on plan formulations and processes may well be a turn in the right direction. But is it realistic if the stringent head-counting of administrators persists? Again, time will show.

Peter Westland is surely right in concluding his epilogue by saying that joint planning is for optimists and realists, but is a frustration if it is carried on as a marginal activity. I will end by a quotation from a letter sent to me by a health administrator after the conference: 'So far as staff attitudes are concerned, they have been one of the greatest sources of strength in the whole transfer (from large central psychiatric hospitals to local arrangements). Without their general sense of the need for a wider range of choice and that the new services generally are much better than the old, the progress we have made so far could not have been achieved merely by central management initiative'. If such readiness exists, then perhaps joint planners can and should be optimistic.

COMMUNITY CARE - A LOCAL AUTHORITY VIEW

John Chant
Director of Social Services, Somerset

Over the past six weeks I have spent on average two evenings per week talking to either worried relatives or anxious staff about a draft strategy to close long-stay hospitals, which has been drawn up in response to the Government's policy of setting targets for the closure of such hospitals.

After 25 years of discussion, one can understand the sense of frustration that prompts Ministers to set targets against which progress and achievement can be measured. But social policy decisions made on the hoof, as it were, are littered with unintended consequences which give rise to hurt, distress, and feelings of impotence on the part of those the policy is designed to support.

At one of our recent meetings of some 300 relatives and interested other parties, an elderly lady explained, in a quiet, dignified manner, that she was 77 years of age, that she had a mentally handicapped daughter whom she had cared for at home for 27 years and that for the last 28 years the daughter had been in hospital. She told the audience that she was happy and content with the placement and felt secure about the arrangements for her daughter's care. She gestured to her elderly husband sitting next to her and said, 'My husband is 83 years old. Will somebody please tell us how we are to approach our death with all the uncertainty we must now face about how and where our daughter is to be cared for?' The meeting rose to support her; people who didn't speak cried, people who did speak were angry and outraged. The hurt of the past and the uncertainty of the future are both incised by targets for closure.

6

It is important that we should help Ministers to understand that the rate of closure of hospitals must be determined by the rate of the development of alternative patterns of service provision. It is in that direction that targets should be set. The service will then be demand-led and our meetings will be with people who are demanding to know why their relatives are not being cared for in community-based facilities.

Whilst professionals and policy-makers have strong reservations about institutional forms of care, it should be clearly understood that many families have yet to place their confidence in alternative community-based models of care. There is a real danger that the whole credibility of community-based systems of care will be undermined by the piecemeal way in which services are being allowed/encouraged to develop. There is a host of evidence to support the view that both mentally handicapped and mentally ill people can gain a great deal from being cared for in domestic settings within the community, but we have still to get that model of care systemised and properly co-ordinated to deliver the services needed for a whole community over more than one generation of need.

It is important that services are developed in the context of both current and future needs.

(i) Proposals must ensure, for instance, that the totality of resources currently deployed to address the needs of mentally handicapped people are secured against their needs, however differently they may be used;

(ii) services must be properly and effectively co-ordinated with the right balance of day, residential and domiciliary care pitched at a level appropriate to the needs of the clients;

(iii) levels of care to severely handicapped people must be improved and the service network must be open to the needs of a new generation of handicapped people;

(iv) local authorities need to act boldly if they are not to find themselves left with the problem without the resources to cope with it.

These parameters argue for a much clearer articulation of the responsibilities which should be assumed by various authorities if a credible service is to be achieved. So-called joint management, or consensus management, does not deliver the goods in terms of establishing a credible service. This should not be taken, however, to indicate a negative attitude towards the value of using a multi-disciplinary base to review the functioning of a particular unit and to ensure that the service it provides remains in line with the requirements of the people who need to use it.

There is a need:

(i)   for clearer definition, integration and articulation of policies for the development of community care at a national level;

(ii)   for the establishment of a financial mechanism which will allow the transfer of resources to develop community-based services;

(iii)   for the development of manpower policies to facilitate and support staff in the transitional arrangement to more community-based care.

Currently, relationships between local government and central government are poor. This has implications for the development of community-based services. Whilst difficulties are most acute where political differences are at their greatest, poor relationships between the two levels of government exist across the spectrum of political views. Relationships are deteriorating as the struggle over resource allocation grows. This deterioration in relationships between central and local government has a particular significance for the personal social services and will impact on the way in which these services can be delivered to the field.
Unlike other services in the local authority setting, the personal social services must mesh into a broad interface with both the health service and the income maintenance services which are directly managed by the Department of Health and Social Security. The need for integrated planning between the three arms of these services, in relation to the development of community care, is self-evident.
Significant development of services cannot take place unless more resources are made available and those additional resources are protected from the general reduction in local authority expenditure. Neither of these things can happen unless at a political level the Government gives leadership and clear direction

to local authorities and secures their co-operation in carrying through agreed programmes.

The new managerialism - performing to targets

Recent ministerial initiatives imply that a new impetus is being given to policies designed to secure the closure of long-stay hospitals for the mentally ill and the mentally handicapped by setting closure dates for such institutions. In the south-west region, target dates have been agreed between the Regional Health Authority and the responsible minister to close eleven long-stay hospitals. The publicly announced aim is to halve the population of these hospitals within five years and to close them in ten years. This announcement was made without any prior consultation with local authorities within the region, and without any indication to the local authority associations at national level that firm targets and objectives were going to be set in this way. The theory is assumed to be, that targets, like hanging, concentrate the mind.

Ironically, these announcements were made just two months after the Somerset Social Services Committee and the Somerset Health Authority had given approval to a jointly agreed plan to move to a further stage of development of services for mentally handicapped people. These plans which will enable the discharge of a minimum of a further 120 and a possible 160 patients over five years, were approved on the basis of a judgement of what could be realistically achieved within the existing climate of resource constraints.

Whilst conjuring up a target date for closure of long-stay hospitals has the impact of concentrating people's thinking, the benefits must be weighed against the damage that is done to staff and morale and commitment. There are major implications, ranging from planning blight to the maintenance of buildings and staff recruitment. Setting dates that are not realistically achievable may be evidence of conviction and determination, but is unlikely to result in sound and purposeful management of such a complex task.

The process of regional review, together with the appointment of general managers on short contracts, is clearly designed to make the performance of the Health Service more responsive to direction. Service objectives will increasingly be targeted and one of the performance criteria against which general managers are likely to be judged will be their success in meeting those targets.

The setting of dates for the closure of long-stay hospitals takes on a particular significance in such arrangements. Setting a date for closure begs the question of whether the goal is to close the hospital or to develop a comprehensive range of community-based services which result in the hospital being no longer required. Social Services Departments and many staff employed in the Health Service are concerned to emphasise that community care is not simply about discharging people from hospital, it is about helping them to re-establish themselves as participating members of the community. The objective must be to avoid institutionalisation and dependency, wherever that is possible.

Community care is a term that should be defined in a positive sense: it must say something about the nature of the care that should be provided in the community. It must not be allowed to become a low-cost strategy for the abandonment of people in need, by decanting them from long-stay hospital into cheap lodgings and the isolated life of a wayfarer.

The term community care should be used to describe a commitment to provide services to support families and informal carers wherever possible, to use substitute family care where the family is unable or unwilling to make provision, and to use admission to hospital and residential care only where absolutely necessary. Those who are admitted to hospital as patients need regular assessment, rehabilitation and, where appropriate, access to training to enable their discharge. The prime purpose must be to prevent people being admitted to hospital inappropriately because of a breakdown in their network of family and social care. Programmes must respect and value the needs of individuals and give opportunity for choice and independence. They must assume that the least restrictive alternative in relation to the needs of an individual will guide the placement that is used and the service which is provided.

Choosing priorities - support and abandonment

Accepting the reality that service provision must inevitably be constrained by availability of resources, difficult choices must be made. Such choices may involve deciding to focus resources on the needs of one group of people to the exclusion of the needs of another. The alternative of spreading resources thinly to everybody may result in services which are ineffective.

Most authorities will define the first priority as the need to develop services to prevent the unnecessary admission of people to hospital. Already in the community there are large numbers of mentally handicapped people being cared for by elderly parents.

The level, range and distribution of day-care resources and programmes are a key element to the build-up of community-based programmes of care. In particular, it is important that those families caring for the most severely handicapped are provided with day care which, given the degree of handicap, is likely to be in special care units. There is scope for day-care programmes to become more community-based. Greater efforts should be made to help people who need such facilities to become involved and to participate in ordinary everyday experiences in the community. More and more they will need to experience the opportunity to give and contribute and not solely to receive care.

The provision of community-based residential care units for children, together with resources to provide short-term and crisis care facilities, can effectively reduce the level of new cases entering hospital-based care systems. But children become adults remarkably quickly; we already have our first generation of leavers who need more adult facilities.

Thus far, the strategies are relatively easy to define and implement. However, without additional resources there comes a point where a clear choice has to be made between developing services to support people in the communities in which they are already living or using those same resources to develop policies to allow large-scale closure of hospitals. Obviously there is some measure of overlap, and a great deal of ingenuity has been used to enable significant numbers of people to leave hospital. However, the core of the problem cannot be addressed without additional resources.

To release the resources locked up in large hospitals, a double banking of expenditure must occur in the initial years to provide the facilities which are needed to allow closure to take place. The first thirty or forty people to leave hospital make little impact on reducing the cost of services provided by the health services but require, both in capital and revenue terms, significant expenditure by the local authorities.

Recently, imaginative attempts have been made to break the deadlock of resource transfer by using the provision of the 1983 'Care in the Community' circular to transfer an annual sum reflecting the average cost per patient place from Health Service expenditure to Social Services expenditure. Increasingly this method is viewed as a possible solution to the growing problems which face local authorities in taking up the joint financing paper, and the objections which local authority associations have to accepting earmarked funds from central government.

The idea is attractively simple; you transfer the patient together with a sum equal to the cost of his/her care from hospital to the community. As and when the consequent services are well established in three to five years, a central book-keeping transfer of funds from the National Health Service budget to the rate-support grant is effected in confirmation of the transfer which has already taken place at operational level.

The solution may be too simple. The implications need to be clearly understood. Transferring resources based on average care costs assumes that responsibility for the total range of care is being transferred. Our own work in drawing up plans to facilitate the discharge of all patients from long-stay hospital provision would suggest that, if Social Services were to assume responsibility for all the low-dependency patients currently resident in the hospital, this would transfer responsibility for 33 per cent of the patient population, but would only release some 10 per cent of the revenue spent on staff. If, in addition, Social Services accepted responsibility for providing care in the community for medium-dependency patients, they would have 70 per cent of the present patient population but would only free approximately 40 per cent of the expenditure spent on staff. Average costs can be misleading and even substantial progress toward placement in the community may not unlock the resources locked into the coffers of institutional care.

It is important therefore, that there should be a clear understanding between Health and Social Services about what their long-term objectives are. There needs to be clear understanding about the care arrangements for those who have maximum dependency. There must be agreement about who is to take the primary responsibility for development, and a recognition of the fact that the economics of the process are likely to determine that there will be a point in the process when it has to be accelerated to contain escalating unit costs of care.

Planning and development
Building services between large organisations to meet the needs of individuals in a way which fits in with local cultural patterns is a complex task. Making things happen in terms of service delivery and influencing patterns of professional practice is difficult and must not be confused with the easier task of agreeing plans between managers who are not directly involved in patient care.

The recent reorganisation of the Health Service has both interrupted and added to the complexities of planning between the Health Service and the Personal Social Services. As a result of reorganisation, there are many areas where there are greater problems in relation to the lack of geographical co-terminosity between the authorities responsible for the provision of the Personal Social Services, the Housing Authorities, and Health Districts. It has taken many Health Authorities longer than anticipated to complete changes of personnel and in a number of areas this has created a hiatus in joint planning arrangements.

In some areas Health Authorities are pursuing detailed plans to establish community-based systems of care for people who are disabled by mental handicap or chronic mental illness, without any significant development of such services by the involvement of the local authority. It is not known whether this reflects an inability or unwillingness to plan and develop service together or whether it reflects the anxieties and concerns of staff currently employed in long-stay hospitals about their future. The fact that such plans appear to be implemented with the approval of Regional Health Authorities highlights the need for structure, collaborative and integrated planning and decision-making arrangements.

There is a danger of services being developed in a competitive rather than a collaborative way. This could result in a mis-match between needs and resources, a lack of clarity about prime areas of responsibility, and unnecessary duplication and wasteful use of resources. Any change involving a reduction of the role of a long-standing institution requires clear aims, strong commitment, careful consultation and determination. Without these there will always be enough ambiguity, prejudice and vested interest to maintain the status quo. The closure of institutions with long history and tradition needs to be done with due regard to, and recognition of, the service commitment which the institution and its staff have given over the years. In the same way that it is necessary to establish a team to commission a new hospital the closure of hospitals in a constructive way is an even more complex task. The idea of de-commissioning teams would be worth careful exploration.

Whilst the general objectives to be achieved in service development and the strategic resource parameters are appropriately set within national and regional forums, we would argue that the detailed plans of service development must be drawn up jointly at a level common to the authorities most directly involved. It is important to ensure that strategic decisions are taken jointly, as it is only in this way that there can be an effective and equal commitment to the outcome. To this end members of Regional Health Authorities need opportunities to meet and agree policies with the elected members of local authorities.

13

Implications for staff

The common experience of both the Health Service and the Personal Social Services is that high standards of care can be provided only if the right calibre of staff are recruited, trained, appreciated and rewarded. We are in danger of overlooking the needs of staff in transition.

There is plenty of evidence to suggest that the shape and form of service provision is as much influenced by attitudes and prejudice as it is by notions of needs and rights. Attempts at joint training are proceeding all too slowly. More thought needs to be given to mechanisms which will facilitate the movement of staff between various settings. The special pension arrangements of staff who work as mental health officers in long-stay hospitals, and the recruitment processes of local government that require staff not previously employed in this service to complete a probationary year, are two particular examples of the problems which can face experienced members of staff in moving from working in a hospital-based setting to community-based services.

Plans to close hosptials will require manpower policies, setting clear options for staff and ensuring that their interests are protected in transition. It is important to acknowledge that there are resources of skill and experience which must also be devolved from the institutional setting. Greater efforts should be made to provide joint training for staff from both the Health and Personal Social Services.

Central to these issues is the need to establish some clear measure of agreement between service organisations as to where primary responsibilities will lie. The broad consensus within social services would lead to the view that the problems which beset mentally handicapped people are primarily social/educational rather than medical, and for this reason we would take the view that the social services infrastructure should be the base upon which services for mentally handicapped people should be developed. The successful treatment and rehabilitation of those who suffer from mental illness, however, will require a primary involvement of medically-based psychiatric services and the social services provisions must be built up in support of the strategies adopted by the psychiatric services.

The preferred solution is, therefore, that, rather than specifically imposing or transferring duties to local authorities, the responsibilities of the Health Service, and the other services on the boundaries, should be more clearly defined by legislation or by other government action. This would be similar to what has already happened in relation to the housing of homeless persons. The 1977 act more clearly defined the responsibilities of District Councils, thus rationalising responsibilities for housing people in need and more clearly defining the residual role of local authorities for social care. A similar approach should be adopted by the National Health Service in defining the limits to which it will exercise responsibilities for mentally handicapped people, the mentally ill, and the elderly. As can probably be gauged from some of the above arguments, the preferred direction of such definition would withdraw the boundaries for mentally handicapped and elderly patients to the provision of acute medical treatment only, but extend them into community support for the mentally ill.

Conclusions

This networking of services can proceed in a positive way, but there comes a point in the evolution of such arrangements when the services and support have to be effectively managed and co-ordinated to ensure that people's needs do not get lost or overlooked. At that point, the issues outlined in this paper will need to be addressed by members of all authorities, by service directors, by field managers and by practitioners. The individual commitment of consultants, nurses and social workers is unlikely to surmount these problems. Failure to seek solutions to these issues in a constructive way will frustrate the vocation of the staff who actually provide the care for people in need. It is likely to lead to a costly and ill-defined service which lacks leadership and direction. Failure to identify solutions is likely to result in long-stay hospitals remaining open for many more years than is currently envisaged, facing even greater problems than they do now in maintaining satisfactory standards of care. Planning is also a doing activity. We must work at these issues if they are not to block progress and distort the provision of services.

A HEALTH SERVICE PERSPECTIVE

P.A. Hunt
Director, National Association of Health Authorities

Unlike the author of the previous paper, and many attending the seminar, I am not a practitioner in the art of Care in the Community and I see my role here as reflecting many of the concerns which have been expressed to the Association by health authorities about the implementation of the Care in the Community policy. I shall also reflect on some of the discussions that have arisen in the joint working party between the DHSS, the NAHA, the Association of Metropolitan Authorities and the Association of County Councils in this area of concern.

May I make it clear that, though I have been asked to concentrate on the problems facing health authorities, I do not want to appear to be too negative. There are many thousands of people who, as a result of Care in the Community policies, have moved out from institutionalised care into the community and who are well supported by statutory and voluntary agencies, where necessary.

That is an achievement we should keep in mind, because I have detected in the last year or so a change in attitude towards Care in the Community policies. More and more questions are being asked about the effectiveness of these policies. These questions have their positive aspect. We should be concerned about what the user of the service actually gets out of the policy, and we should not be surprised to see a reaction against statutory agencies which are seen as being happy to reduce hospital places for mentally ill and mentally handicapped people whilst not providing the necessary support for these people actually entering

16

the community. But this attitude has its negative side. I fear that the lack of proper community facilities is being used in some places as an excuse for holding up progress; for keeping hospitals open and for not taking the hard management decisions that I believe are necessary. And it would be tragic if we were to suffer a loss of nerve over Care in the Community policies at this stage.

Where have we got to?

The number of patients in long-stay hospitals has reduced quite considerably in the last few years. Between 1979 and 1983 the number of people resident in a mental handicap hospital or unit fell by 12 per cent to 40,200. In mental illness hospitals and units, the numbers fell by 10 per cent to 69,000. But, as John Chant inferred, it is interesting to note that DHSS Ministers have on more than one occasion expressed frustration at the lack of hospital closures. Only 2 were approved for closure in 1982, 6 in 1983 and 14 in 1984. And only about half of these have already closed and some that have not will stay open for several years.

What has happened to the people who have left our long-stay hospitals? As I said before, many are now living very successfully in the community, but others are not. The evidence given to the Social Services Select Committee on this point is illuminating. It revealed:

(i) the phenomenon of mentally disturbed people living grim lives in boarding houses;

(ii) the number of inappropriate discharges from hospitals that are taking place when no real support exists in the community to care for the patient;

(iii) the fact that a Psychiatric Rehabilitation Association survey found that of long-stay hospital patients discharged from hospital in one year, as many as 40 per cent of the sample had no contact with the hospital or social services;

(iv) that what is described as Care in the Community is often not that. Are the hostels or units of 15 to 25 beds really domestic settings or are they an institutionalised small hospital? And the Social Services Committee found examples of new units on the 15/25 bed model still being planned and constructed.

As regards day care for the mentally ill, the Select Committee was struck by the appalling inadequacy of day-care facilities for those suffering from, recovering from, or liable to a recurrence of mental illness.

The Committee felt that the pace of removal of hospital facilities has far outrun the provision of services in the community to replace them, that obsessive concentration on mechanisms for getting people out of hospital has sometimes obscured the fact that most mentally ill or handicapped people already live in the community, and that the fate of those already living outside hospitals has been neglected.

So who is responsible for the present situation?

Many people can be held responsible:

- the Government for raising expectations which could not be met, for suggesting that Care in the Community was a straightforward operation which could be paid for on a self-financing basis;

- health and social service authorities for not working together or providing the leadership and commitment needed to tackle the complexities of community care;

- hospital staff who feel their jobs are under threat;

- the present economic recession which has made local authorities reluctant to make available the necessary resources;

- suspicion on the part of health authorities that local authorities will use money given to them by the NHS in an inappropriate way.

You can take your pick from these and others. For my part, I would start with the key relationship between health and local authorities. We know it is not always what it should be. The following comment in the Health Advisory Service 1984 Annual Report could be applied to a considerable extent to all user groups:

Changes in mental illness services can only be achieved by co-operation between health authorities, local authority social services, housing authorities and voluntary bodies. It is disappointing to find repeatedly that although care staff from all these agencies find ways to work together in the interests of their clients, their respective parent organisations fail to

18

develop jointly owned policies. Lack of co-terminosity, differing financial time-tables and conflicting priorities all play their part. Joint finance monies are all too often used to plug service deficiencies rather than to initiate change where it is needed. With a few exceptions, health authorities have so far been reluctant to transfer funds under the 'Care in the Community' label for the re-orientation of mental illness services. All too frequently, discussions about finance between the authorities obscure the far more important need to develop jointly agreed plans.

Confusion about division of responsibilities

The development of joint plans is often easier said than done. Confusion about responsibility for service provision is frequent. Some local authorities have been very backward in providing community support. Health authorities keen to reduce hospital provision are filling the vacuum with health services facilities in the community, sometimes without adequate consultation with local authorities and without full consideration of whether clients' needs might not be better met by social services provision.

Many problems arise in the case of those hospitals whose patients are drawn from a wide number of local authorities. For such a hospital to have to relate to a large number of District Health Authorities and local authorities if patients are to be discharged successfully, the organisational and financial difficulties are immense.

Lack of co-terminosity

Lack of co-terminosity is crucial. The 1982 reorganisation of the NHS disrupted joint planning arrangements over much of the country. Although formal structures have quickly been re-established, relationships between health and local authorities are now inevitably more complex in the majority of areas. If there are several DHAs within one local social services authority's area they may for good reasons adopt quite different approaches to service development.

Some local social services authorities have decentralised the operational management of social services, but this does not necessarily make the task of joint planning easier where authority to reach agreement is not delegated to divisional managers. DHAs have found that decisions made at divisional level are being referred back to County Hall and the bureaucracy involved becomes enormous.

Because of the 1982 changes, Loughborough University and the National Association of Health Authorities (NAHA) conducted a survey of all DHAs to ascertain how far a basic framework of collaborative machinery had been established two years after restructuring (31 March 1984). This showed that substantial gaps existed in the planning machinery of priority care groups and that relatively few 'problem-solving' mechanisms existed - only 20 per cent of Joint Care Planning Team groups had been given a specific task and only 31 per cent had fixed time limits placed on their work. Gaps in the planning machinery for priority care groups meant that substantially less than half of all localities produced jointly agreed strategies for any of those groups between 1982 and 1984.

What about joint consultative committees?

Ask a health authority member his or her view of such Committees and I think many of them will say that they act as rubber-stamps for approving joint finance applications and little more. Many meet only one a year. Indeed, the role of health authority and local authority members ought to be one of very great value, but I believe they have not used their leadership role to the extent required.

Resources

Resources are of course a major problem. The Social Services Select Committee said in their report: 'It is widely accepted that an overall higher real level of funding of resources for mentally ill or handicapped people is necessary.'

Uncertainty about future resources is itself a major obstacle. I believe that without arrangements for bridging finance, possibly involving a special regional or central allocation, real change is very difficult. There can be substantial transitional costs in the switch from hospital care, since existing services must continue to operate while new services are built up. Moreover, savings do not accrue in full until the old facilities are completely closed.

And although joint finance arrangements have made a valuable contribution towards paying for Care in the Community, as well as in promoting joint planning, this is not the answer. Indeed, taking the total budgets of NHS and social services, joint finance is purely marginal. And even then health authorities frequently complain that local authorities are reluctant to embark on joint finance programmes with long-term revenue consequences, because of uncertainties about future resources.

Other problems

There are other important reasons for some of the problems we have identified. There are the obstacles stemming from the attitudes and relationships of individuals: for example, different perceptions of priorities; different professional traditions and perceived status; the natural concern of staff about the effect of changes on jobs. But I suspect that many of those attending the seminar are in a better position to talk about that than myself. We know the problem of staff who have been trained to work in hospital and are often not prepared to work in the community, preferring the security of a familiar setting. Staff do feel threatened by change; unless their job security, future prospects, pensions and status are safeguarded, staff resistance can impede the implementation of care in the community.

Conclusion

Although there are many problems, we must not allow ourselves to be drawn into a position where they are felt to be insurmountable, because we have no alternative. Care in the Community is here to stay. There is no going back to our large longstay NHS institutions. We have to believe that the financial and organisational problems can be overcome and that the system can cater for the needs of each individual use of the service. And that is the challenge to which the other papers will be addressing themselves.

POTENTIALITIES AND LIMITATIONS OF THE PRESENT ARRANGEMENTS

R. Hampson, K.Judge, J. Renshaw
Personal Social Services Research Unit, University of Kent

The Government launched its Care in the Community initiative in 1983 and pilot projects under its umbrella have been funded since April 1984. The Personal Social Services Research Unit has been commissioned to promote the initiative and to monitor and evaluate the projects. The DHSS selected thirteen projects in the first round and has now chosen a further fifteen for the second round, which began in April 1985.

The aim of the initiative is to help long-stay hospital patients kept in hospital unnecessarily to return to the community, if this will be best for them and is what they and their families prefer. In 1981 the consultative document 'Care in the Community' sought views on various ways of easing the movement of people from hospital into community care. It was followed in 1983 by a circular of the same name, which set out a number of decisions following from those consultations. The basis for financial collaboration between District Health Authorities and local authorities was improved. DHAs are now able to make extended payments from their normal funds to help the move to community care. The qualifying conditions and time periods for joint finance itself have been extended in relation to projects for transfers from hospital to community care, and DHAs are now able to support education and housing for handicapped people.

On top of that, about £20 million was added to joint finance funds over five years particularly to boost the Care in the Community initiative. Most of this has been reserved to help fund the programme of pilot projects.

The pilot projects are intended to launch the initiative, explore and evaluate different approaches to moving people and resources into community care, and build up experience which will then be disseminated. Projects are designed to identify and meet the needs of long-stay hospital patients who can be moved into the community. Those needs must be specified and assessed in advance, and the wishes of patients and their families taken into account. Up to 100 per cent funding may be sought for capital or revenue expenditure or both. Revenue support is made available for each project selected for a period of three years on the understanding that the project will continue with local funding after that time if it is successful.

Projects deal with a variety of services catering for those who need different degrees of support and care. These include residential care and day-care provision and support services for families. Projects range in size from those which will involve a hundred or more patients, and those which cater for only a dozen. The large projects all intend to make broad structural changes to the nature of the total service offered locally to the client group concerned.

The aim is to investigate how cost-effective community services can be provided to meet the needs of the various different groups of long-stay hospital patients. A thousand such people, elderly, mentally ill, and mentally handicapped, are now involved in the projects.

The PSSRU evaluation looks at each project to discover how it works, what it costs, and whether it improves the well-being of clients. An integral part of the evaluation will therefore be a costing exercise, largely of the community facilities set up or tapped into by the projects. But equally important will be an assessment of the financial structure of projects and of how they mesh into local and national political economies.

Finance and structure of the Care in the Community initiative

It would be a mistake to prejudge the results of the evaluation of the pilot projects: the aim is not only to move clients into the community, but to do so in a cost-effective manner which can be repeated by others. Many of the most important lessons to be learned will be to do with the relative success of different kinds of individual community placement. In the nature of the case, this information can only fully emerge over a period of years. In particular, the costing exercise which is a major part of the PSSRU evaluation cannot be the subject of this paper: there are as yet no results from it.

A central part of the DHSS rationale for the programme has been to fund projects which look as if they will improve clients' lives and also as if, if successful, they are affordable and therefore replicable by other authorities. Moreover, one part of any funding calculation must be the savings that may be made at the hospital end, and indeed the possibility in some places of selling off sites. But few people involved in getting new or extended community services off the ground find it easy to believe that they can be wholly or largely financed by hospital savings, and that is not regarded as the central thrust of the programme.

The definition of the economic costs of the move towards community care is, however, only one interest of the DHSS and the policy world in general. At least as important is a more institutional concern with how financial packages are put together to facilitate the move, and with the administrative and budgetary effects of changes in service delivery practices. The evaluation of the initiative hopes also to make useful statements about these policy questions, and even at this stage it is possible to make some interim statements.

Institutions

The financial packages funding the twenty-eight projects have been put together by a variety of different agencies and combinations of agencies. They are roughly identifiable as those which are either Health instigated, Social Services instigated, or Voluntary instigated, and those which have arisen out of Joint Working or some other kind of coalition. Since inter-agency co-operation is a condition of receipt of central funding (through the Joint Finance mechanism) and also virtually unavoidable in the nature of the case, the extent to which projects can be single agency affairs once they are off the mark is limited: nevertheless, they have often been largely germinated in one agency, and some continue to have only minimal input from other agencies, or added impetus only from one other agency.

The Chichester mental illness project, for instance, was very much a Health project, devised by professionals and administrators in Graylingwell Hospital and the DHA. Together they planned the outline of rehabilitation in the hospital and took their ideas far enough to be able to give a coherent remit to a housing association for the facilities which will be needed by both patients and the Community Rehabilitation Team, which will effectively move out of hospital with the patients. The Maidstone project arose in the first instance out of a desire in Kent Social Services to replicate for mentally handicapped people the successful approach developed in the Community Care Scheme for the elderly.

On the other hand, in Torbay, for example, a voluntary agency, the Parkview Society, directed by a coalition of representatives from all concerned local agencies, and thus able to draw on resources from all of them and to plead its case easily through local joint bodies, had cut its teeth on setting up a hostel for mentally ill people and now proposes to do so for those with a mental handicap. Although superficially a Voluntary enterprise, this is clearly a case of genuine joint working, with enough entrepreneurial flair to make use of the Social Security budget to meet local needs.

The resulting projects are managed, once they have been set in motion, by a variety of other combinations of agencies and indeed new agencies. All of these are in one sense or another constrained not merely by the amount of their funding, but also by the methodology it imposes. Maidstone, most obviously, applies a well-worked-out set of economic principles to service delivery itself.

Finance
Funding packages have a number of different component parts:

i)   Bridges.   All the Care in the Community projects, by definition, are taking some short-term funds (from the DHSS) as what has elegantly been termed 'hump money'. Crudely speaking, £16 million of central hump money is involved in the move of 1,000 clients out of hospital over three years. This figure does, however, include some capital expenditures for facilities with a much longer life, and of course all the clients make use of existing facilities and other budgets. Several projects use other available district or regional sources, like the North West Regional Health Authority's bridging fund for mental handicap services. It ought also to be said that virtually none of these budgets are 'bridging funds' in the ordinary sense, that is, money laid out to cover a temporary shortfall and to be repaid later. They are actually sinking funds.

ii)   Deals.   A range of sources of funds are combined in about 28 different ways in the programme as a whole: first, to fund whatever is needed to rehabilitate pilot project clients and support them in the community on top of the hump money, second, to maintain those people in the community after the three-year pilot project, and third, to underwrite a continuing flow from the hospitals outside the scope of, and after, the pilot project.

The sources include:

<u>Direct pick-up</u>: the agency which ends up providing the service picks up the tab. Social Services pay for the social worker, and so on. This is true for some part of every project.

<u>Indirect payment</u>: some parts of the project are financed by the agency of origin, or by a third party who feels responsible. These funds include regional revenue; regional capital; transfer between Districts; transfer from local District to Social Services; transfer from a distant District to Social Services, either because a hospital of origin is in the outlying District or because patients 'belong' to the outlying District; transfers from Districts to voluntary organisations.

Such transfers may be within or outside the Joint Finance mechanism. What is interesting is not merely the range of sources, but also the species of deal which is struck in each case. Transfers may be 'dowry payments' which recur annually for some time, or one-off lump sums. They may be calculated on the basis of actual savings made in hospital, as in Derby, or on an estimate of average or marginal hospital costs, as at Maidstone, or on the extra cost to the final agency of some specific extra service that will have to be provided. At Warwick for instance the Social Services Department have produced a notional average costing for Social Education Centre places which clients will need. The District will transfer an equivalent amount to MENCAP with each client. MENCAP will use it to buy SEC places for those who need them from the SSD.

iii) <u>Other budgets</u>. Supplementary, Housing and other benefits are of course a major source of finance for community care. Many clients in the programme receive Supplementary Benefit in the normal way, in effect as the replacement for the hotel costs previously picked up by the hospital. But several projects make 'creative' use of these budgets, that is, they use them in ways national policy-makers may not have intended, and may in some cases be a little uneasy about. The national position here has changed already during the initiative, and may well change again.

A particularly disturbing feature of the most recent change is the extent to which the new Supplementary Benefit rules may be thought to hinder 'normalisation'. The rates of benefit are now scaled in a way which financially penalises those who live on their own, away from paid carers.

Some projects also tap into the housing funding mechanism, especially through the Housing Corporation.

Discussion

A number of points need to be made. First, 'savings' in a hospital are never simply objective facts. They are administrative agreements, subject to a range of institutional and political pressures. They cause changes in the level and style of services just as much as they result from them.

Second, the main element both in the definition of hospital savings, and then in what is done with them, is the simple conflict of interest over whether the 'gain' should accrue inside or outside the hospital. Health professionals are bound to prefer spending the same amount on fewer patients rather than depleting already inadequate budgets - to spread out the beds rather than close wards, as it were. One of the Care in the Community projects, Kidderminster, explicitly aims to develop and improve its hospital services for mentally handicapped people alongside its community programme, using what is saved by closing Lea Hospital to help fund both arms of the strategy. In a number of other projects there is strong reason to suppose that, although solid agreements to transfer funds will be met, the running down of real resources on which hospital administrators have predicated their agreement to lose finance may prove mysteriously difficult to realise: there will be a funding transfer not really matched by a reduction in what hospitals actually plan to do.

Third, Social Services Departments suffer from a particular twist of the most basic distinction, between cost-effectiveness and cheapness. It is now reasonable to suppose that there do exist whole sets of feasible packages for making cost-effective moves from hospital to community care. The community packages will usually be more expensive, but society in principle regards that extra expense as much more than matched by the benefits which accrue, largely but by no means wholly to the clients. That, however, still leaves SSD managers having to find the actual cash difference. In the nature of the case, even average long-term hospital savings may well not be enough. This is where the Supplementary Benefits budget has come in. But the Short Committee's view, that an excessive reliance on social security payments may threaten the long-term stability of the care system, ought surely to be given the most careful consideration.

The emerging pattern

Thus there begins to be a picture of the arrangements that have been made by local and district managers, the constraints they have arisen from, and the service aims they have produced. We can now add to that an interim view of some of the difficulties, first at the local level, thereafter more globally, that these plans are meeting, and of what steps practitioners would perhaps be best advised to take against the dangers.

First the local picture.

Agency issues

The local climate of joint working and co-operation before a project is even mooted is a key factor in its future success. Political commitment of the relevant agencies to the new project is equally important. This is true both in the obvious sense, that the directly sponsoring agencies should be energetically committed, and also in the less direct sense, that other agencies whose willingness to participate can make or break the venture should be fully involved. For instance, a Housing Department should be aware of when and where it may be asked to contribute.

There are special difficulties when the project aims to move clients to a Social Services area which is outside the Health Authority area of the hospital from which the clients start. Although local joint working in the receiving area may be excellent, with the best will in the world misunderstandings are likely to occur between authorities which have not previously had diplomatic relations, let alone the degree of co-operation at the client level needed to instigate proper services.

Project issues

There are a number of problems which arise simply from the fact that projects are developed within the somewhat artificial framework of a pilot programme. In the first place, although quite detailed outline plans had to be produced in order to win central funding, only those few first-round projects which were planning to go ahead anyway, by raising the money elsewhere, were in a position to forge ahead the minute they knew their proposal had been accepted. Others had to gear themselves up with the operational planning which could not sensibly be done on the off-chance of winning.

Secondly, both rounds of projects have inevitably had what, in the context of the usual planning horizons of health and local authorities, has been extremely short notice that they were to be funded at all. Long lead-in times are needed to set up the machinery to identify and assess patients, and to provide new services and facilities or at least adapt existing provision.

Thirdly, the finance arrangements for the Care in the Community initiative are severe constraints. Having been provisionally allocated sums over three fiscal years, projects are required to use the money within precisely that period: they cannot allow their spending to spill over into fourth or later years. The combination of this with the practical absence of any project at all in the first weeks of funding, for the reasons already mentioned, has made life difficult for many a senior project manager.

Projects have also, however, had problems other than those predictably consequent on a date-stamped initiative, and those to do with the time which has to be invested in the implementation of any safe change in people's lives. Building or adapting premises for hostels, day centres, and other facilities, for instance, has almost universally taken longer than originally envisaged. This does seem largely to stem from over-sanguine expectations about the ability of builders and planners to deliver the goods promptly. And perhaps, to a lesser extent, from a similar over-optimism about how long the search for suitable sites and premises would take.

Attracting qualified staff has also been unexpectedly vexatious in many areas. New community nurses, social workers, psychologists, have all been slow to materialise, and in places appointments have simply not been made at all. Why this should be so is not obvious. It may be that the services of good people are so much in demand that they have no need to incur the risks of involvement in short-term funded enterprises. If that is the case, then there are interesting times ahead for project promoters in local, health, and perhaps most of all in voluntary and private agencies. Such short-term posts do seem to be making up an increasing share of the labour market for these kinds of staff. If the middle rank commands which must urgently have to be filled, at the front line of new developments, attract only the staff who cannot find more secure things to do, there will be major hurdles to change in the Welfare State. This situation cries out for local management to be allowed and encouraged to put together flexible incentive packages for new staff.

But this leads naturally to the inverse problem faced in some form by virtually every project - the attitude of existing staff to the new service plans. This is most acute at the hospital end, where nursing and ancillary staff, in particular, can feel resentment and fear towards a community project which they may regard as a threat to their future livelihood. As indeed in many cases it really is. This may be exacerbated by the difference

29

between hospital and field agency cultures, and the different models of care they may hold to.

Furthermore, new staff hired by the recently financed project can have very different views of what it is they are supposed to do from those, usually somewhat more senior, people who have been playing the Pilot Project-Central Funding-Joint Finance game for some time.

Some conclusions

If this paints a somewhat gloomy picture for those - the second round of projects, for instance - who have to set out on this road, then it can already be matched by a number of positive recommendations.

Project co-ordination and management are vital variables

-    Designation of a full- or nearly full-time Co-ordinator at an early stage is enormously helpful.

-    Clear lines of accountability both horizontally and vertically through what are often large unusual coalitions of executive staff must be spelt out, and communication along those lines constantly clarified. New appointees should be inducted very carefully into the ensuing web.

-    A case management and key worker system is a central feature in virtually every successful project, with the concomitant case review and monitoring implications.

-    Projects should produce a management timetable from Day 1, setting out what services they expect to deliver, to which clients, in what facilities, when, and most of all, what has to be done in the intermediate stages to achieve these goals.

Public relations and promotional activity need detailed planning

-    Hospital staff in particular should be carefully but honestly approached, as should the relatives of patients.

-    There are real difficulties in the involvement of clients at early stages of projects. Nevertheless, community care which neglects to involve clients is in real trouble.

-    Planning permission has proved difficult in several projects, and so have more general relations with the public at large. No firm recommendation can be made on whether it is better to go for the low profile - ordinary people don't need to ask permission to move into an ordinary street - approach, or whether the high profile - hold a public meeting - approach is preferable. But there are traps on all sides, which projects ignore at their peril.

Sea-change

Turning now to the more global, macro picture, perhaps the central lesson so far to be learnt from the pilot projects is also the most open to varying political reinterpretation. It clearly is possible for creative innovators to put together packages of services, facilities and agencies which are new at least to the local context in which they take place, and use funds from a variety of sources, sometimes intended by policy-makers for quite different ends. Housing and voluntary associations, for instance, can be prompted by bright personnel from the health or local authority to make interesting use of Supplementary Benefit to provide good new services for small numbers of clients. It is also clear that, however much the non-statutory sector may grow, in any foreseeable future the main responsibility for those of the mentally disabled and elderly who need professional intervention will continue to lie with the statutory agencies. A sea-change in the nature of services to be delivered, as envisaged by all political parties and embodied in the Care in the Community programme, must therefore imply that the huge agencies involved should adapt to the new situation. Inevitable though this is, it will also be gradual. A conflict therefore already exists, and may well grow, between <u>Creative Marginal Intervention</u> and <u>Incremental Adaptation of Large Organisations</u>. Reconciling, or at least diverting, this conflict is a major task for both local and national policy-makers.

A major aspect of that conflict, thrown into a stark light by several of the pilot projects, is that policy-makers, particularly at the local level, need to think hard about the long-term consequences of planning services by response to client needs alone. The professional temptation - some professionals would say obligation - to do this is very great. Nevertheless, as a matter of fact services will always be constrained by available resources. It would seem to follow that if planning to meet clients' needs is increasingly devolved to the key worker level, as many argue that it should be, then so equally should awareness of macro financial constraints, and the ability to plan within them, be devolved.

Service planners and case managers have not been encouraged by the practice and tradition of British social and health policy to develop such cost consciousness. Training is no doubt one part of the answer to this, as is strong managerial direction. But the value of changes in the incentive structure has to be emphasised. The incentives in question are not by any means restricted to perks and pay rises. A clear lesson from the Care in the Community projects, as it has been from the Kent Community Care experiment, is that even very junior staff, and certainly middle rankers, will respond with enthusiasm to the increased responsibilities of devolved planning for services at the client level.

TRANSFERRING RESPONSIBILITY

Tessa Jowell
Assistant Director MIND

No one would have predicted that a surge in the development of locally based mental health services would coincide with a Conservative government which is deeply committed to restraining public expenditure. We are faced, not with just localised flurries of activity, but with an emerging national trend which, on the basis of strategic plans submitted to the DHSS, indicates that over the next ten years thirty of the hundred or so traditional mental hospitals will close. The following factors have undoubtedly played a part in creating this new sense of urgency.

i)   There has been a gradual but slow development of local authority, voluntary organisation and other alternatives to the large mental hospital.   Also an increasingly self-confident professional preference for treatment outside rather than inside the large institution has reduced the numbers of people in mental hospitals.

ii)   District Health Authorities are faced with enormous bills for essential repairs to the crumbling fabric of many of the large mental hospitals.   In many cases the capital cost of repair is equivalent to a substantial development fund for a local mental health service.

iii)   The public debate about the 1983 Mental Health Act has had a spin-off effect in terms of reawakening public concern about conditions in the large mental hospitals.

iv)   Government policy has pushed the development of locally based mental health services as a political priority both through the regional review mechanism and also through the Community Care programme and other smaller-scale initiatives.

But we ought not to be too preoccupied by the causes of the new enthusiasm and commitment to change. More important is the need for the momentum to be maintained to create a national pattern of service for the treatment, care and support of mentally ill people and their families which:

(a)   enhances citizenship for all those who have suffered or are suffering from mental illness;

(b)   reduces or eliminates the inequalities which are inevitably created by the experience of mental illness.

This process of deinstitutionalisation is therefore a humanising trend to reintegrate people into the community, to rebuild fulfilled and autonomous lives, and to provide support appropriate to individual need in meeting this objective. The mental hospitals cannot by their very nature do this and ultimately this is why the argument for their phased closure appears now to have been won. The segregation of people in institutions highlights and reinforces their difference rather than their similarity with the rest of us in the world outside. Institutions are characteristically introspective, providing all service and all support to all residents, contact with the outside world being limited to the odd foray to the local shops, or an outing in a transit van with the hospital name emblazoned on the side. The mental hospital cannot possibly provide a normal social environment; it invites dependence yet reproaches the dependant. But having said this we must never underestimate the service provided to generations of mentally ill people by the hospital system, usually because there was no alternative. The hospital has been a comforting source of reliability and continuity. This is why the replacement of the mental hospital service is mourned by many patients and their carers. The mental hospital has always been a place of refuge in the middle of the night when the local authority day centre is closed, or the emergency duty team is under strength, or the crisis centre set up two years ago has stopped taking new referrals. Most mentally ill people, and indeed their carers, have such low expectations of the mental health service that something is better than nothing at all. The greatest dread is that when the mental hospitals do close there will be nothing at all.

The scepticism about the development of local mental health services shared by patients, families, and staff, and underpinned by public anxiety, is fed by some of the following beliefs that mental hospital replacement means:

i) transfer of responsibility to local government, thereby abandoning a national, if fundamentally mediocre, standard of care for uncertain and sometimes non-existent local authority services;

ii) transfer from professional support to carer;

iii) transfer from hospital to voluntary or private sector care;

iv) transfer from nursing care to social work support.

It is not therefore surprising that much of the hostility and organised opposition to mental hospital closure has come from the trade union and women's movements, both of whom see their 'membership' as being vulnerable to large-scale exploitation if the promises offered by the development of the new service are not fulfilled. There is also a cause for concern among some mental health professionals. Professor Kathleen Jones describes in a recent paper(1) how, when she presented proposals for the generic mental health worker to the Royal College of Psychiatrists, she received a guarded and qualified reaction which was ultimately articulated by one psychiatrist who said, 'We don't want to be mental health professionals, we want to be doctors'!

So although in theory the arguments about the importance of a radical recasting of the mental health services have been won, everybody concerned believes that in some way or other they will be a loser. Patients fear they may be left without treatment and support. Carers fear they will be left to provide the support alone. Hospital staff fear they will lose their jobs. Psychiatrists fear they will lose status and control. How then do we begin to build a sense of what can positively be achieved from this despondence?

The process of upheaval for staff and patients and the uncertainties caused to families impose the greatest obligation to create an alternative which inspires the same faith in terms of its reliability. And that the alternative will mitigate rather than multiply the disabilities caused by recurrent mental illness.

Against this background, therefore, is the issue really about transferring responsibilities? Isn't it really about a more visionary process of service recreation? We are still too dependent on the mental hospital model of service as the point from which we begin to build the alternative. We know from abundant clinical evidence that people with persistent mental illness need not necessarily live in hospital. We have also learnt from the pioneers of local mental health service development that dispersal is by and large a much more effective way of organising the care staff than the conventional centralisation in the mental hospital.

Building the alternative thus involves establishing first of all a number of certainties:

i) For staff. Hospital-based staff must be recruited as allies in the development of the new service. This will only work where a negotiated agreement about the impact on existing jobs is reached at the earliest opportunity.

ii) For carers. Absolute guarantees must be provided that the mental hospital service will continue to operate until the alternative new locally based services are established.

iii) For consumers. The reported unwillingness of patients to move out of the large mental hospitals has often been used as an argument in support of their retention. Consumers must be guaranteed absolute continuity of access to care and support appropriate to their individual needs. They must also be supported in developing an awareness of the alternatives to hospital life and must be allowed to express preferences on the basis of informed choice.

Furthermore an atmosphere of public certainty must be created whereby the public hostility to local mental health services, often characterised by remarks such as 'Will our children be safe on the street?', is dealt with by accurate information and the visibility of service and support as needs arise. The overriding objective in transferring treatment from the large mental hospital base to a dispersed local service is to desegregate mentally ill people. Many of their needs for support are no different from those of the rest of us, providing that this can be augmented by access to specialist services at times of particular need. It is this preoccupation with individuality and a minimum degree of therapeutic intervention consistent with the person's disability that must characterise every aspect of the process of transfer, the planning process, the implementation process and the development process.

Let us now turn to implementing the transfer of resources, the contributors to the process and what they have and should offer. The process of transfer must be planned and the parties to the process must be involved in the planning process. In this way the planning process will act as a preliminary softening-up for the operational stages when a plan is implemented. Successful implementation crucially depends on the development of a shared service culture rather than simply combining the organisational traditions of the members of the planning team. A locally based mental health service is more than simply the sum of health service, local authority, voluntary organisation, private sector, and informal caring systems. The sort of service culture that the planning team should be seeking to create through a range of dispersed local facilities will mean that:

i)   The service will value the client as a full citizen with rights and responsibilities, entitled to be consulted and to have an opportunity actively to shape and influence relevant services, no matter how severe his or her disability.

ii)   The service will aim to promote the greatest self-determination of the client on the basis of informed and realistic choice and will provide and evaluate a programme of treatment, care and support based on his or her unique needs.

iii)   The service will aim to meet the special needs arising from disability through a locally accessible fully co-ordinated multi-disciplinary service operated by appropriately trained staff. The service will be easily accessible locally and delivered wherever possible in the client's usual environment.

It is the permeation of the service culture throughout every facility of the decentralised mental health service that is important. Arguments about apportioning organisational responsibility, particularly as between the health service and local authority services, are almost entirely unproductive. Indeed, in those areas where bold and imaginative initiatives have taken place, i.e. Torbay and Exeter Health Authorities, the initiative has come principally from the nursing profession, often caricatured as the most reactionary and resistant to change. Furthermore, the changing political environment has created a pluralism in the provision of welfare services which must be taken into account as part of service planning.

Whatever the rhetoric may suggest, community care is not care by the community but involves developing a comprehensive local mental health service in the community.

The implementation programme therefore has a number of key points:

i)   an agreed vision of what the new service should look like;

ii)   clear principles on which the description of the new service is based and against which it is evaluated;

iii)   the professional and managerial will to put it into action. Having a plan is not an end in itself, and the importance of the small group of heroic innovators must never be underestimated;

iv)   the political will to make it a reality. This means providing the additional funding to meet the additional costs of transition;

v)   dissemination of information about good models of decentralised service that can be explored by staff during the process;

vi)   staff involvement at all levels in the planning and implementation process;

vii)   consumer user and carer involvement in the planning and implementation process.

So what will the new service look like? It should be characterised by its accessibility and sensitivity to individual need, its local identity, its combination of specialist and generic services. It will be difficult to prescribe one model that will be equally appropriate to the needs of an inner city population and of a dispersed rural area. Buildings will be less in evidence as means of defining the service than under the old pattern of care. Indeed a cautionary reminder is necessary for service planners, not to become diverted by preoccupation with buildings at the cost of the service culture; small hostels can be just as pernicious in promoting institutionalisation as the largest and most remote run-down mental hospital. Parts of the mental health service may therefore be located in unlikely places - the local citizens advice bureau, the local adult education institute or through the resources of the local authority housing department.

But this is not to imply that hospital treatment will have no place in the new service. The difference will be that the hospital sector will not dominate the other services. It will be people's needs rather than the extrapolation of need through DHSS norms that will determine the volume and nature of the service. In the past, service planners and professionals have seen themselves in discrete boxes providing discrete parts of a mental health service. Many 'patients' are 'discharged' from the psychiatric services and 'placed' in private and voluntary homes, ostensibly under the social services department. Whilst some patients, quite rightly, should leave a health service establishment or institution, they should not necessarily be discharged from the mental health service overall. The service should aim to co-ordinate a range of appropriate and professional volunteer workers able to respond to a person's needs in the least segregated environment consistent with that person's disability. This is not to suggest some kind of all-embracing paternalistic service but rather one which to the patient or user seems like a seamless and coherent source of help, fully co-ordinated and delivering care appropriate to needs expressed from time to time. The challenge is to create that seamless co-ordination between disparate agencies with their own style of management in structure, forms of accountability, professional rivalry and so forth.

The balanced service system as developed by John O'Brien, Director of Housing, London Borough of Southwark, recommends classifying services according to their intended impact on the lives of the people they service. The emphasis is on individuality rather than the functional response to need, for example as day-care services or residential services.

There are accordingly seven major service functions:

i)   identification - services aimed at determining the need for, or the establishment of, service relationships between the consumer and the provider;

ii)   crisis stabilisation - services aimed at the reduction of acute mental disability and its physical and social manifestations to ensure the safety of an individual or society;

iii)   growth - services aimed at enhancing intra-personal and inter-personal and instrumental skills;

iv)   sustenance - services aimed at maintaining intra-personal, inter-personal and instrumental skills;

v)   case management - services aimed at linking the service system to the consumer and at co-ordinating the various components of this system to achieve a mutually successful outcome;

vi) <u>prevention</u> - services aimed at reducing the incidence of mental disability resulting from spiritual, social, emotional, intellectual, or biological causes;

vii) <u>domiciliary</u> - services which complement the provision of other services.

The service functions can be seen to be provided in three distinct types of environment:

i) <u>natural</u> - which could be home, workplace, school or other place in the community which provides the least degree of segregation;

ii) <u>supportive</u> - the open access services such as day centres, hostels, workshops and other community-based facilities which provide a moderate degree of structure and control;

iii) <u>protective</u> - hospitals, nursing homes and prisons which provide the highest degree of restriction.

The balanced service system requirements could be implemented through the following facilities:

(a) <u>The local mental health resource centre</u> which would provide secondary care and treatment, through access to a multi-disciplinary professional team, providing day-care, day-hospital and treatment services with beds available for people requiring in-patient care during a period of acute illness. The resource centre would seek to serve a population of between fifty and sixty thousand.

(b) <u>The neighbourhood activity centre</u> which would provide a 24-hour point of access to a multi-disciplinary team to service the disabled person living in his or her own home. It would essentially be the focus for rehabilitation and support for long-term mentally ill people and would provide a service base for key workers such as home helps, voluntary organisation workers, housing officers from housing departments, nurses, social workers and other related staff.

(c) Housing and accommodation. Through this area of activity the major range of accommodation would be provided in a variety of settings ranging from ordinary housing to group homes or small hostels. The housing and accommodation facilities would be linked to the neighbourhood centre and mental health resource centre, offering the opportunity for linking tenants into supportive networks both with each other and with other tenants.

This service structure would clearly be more staff-intensive. Part of the increased need would be met by retraining and relocation of current hospital staff and also by offering retraining and relocation opportunities to some local authority domiciliary staff.

The old adage warns us that 'it is better to travel hopefully than to arrive' and indeed the development of community care policy over the past 20 years has identified a lot of hopeful travel in terms of rhetorical commitment and grand statements of intent. But these have been matched by precious little action. We owe it to the present generation of mentally ill people to deliver the fulfilled promises of past generations.

Footnote
(1) Kathleen Jones, The mental health professional in 2000 AD, unpublished paper delivered to the Inter-disciplinary Association of Mental Health Workers, 1985.

ALTERNATIVE SOLUTIONS: SERVICE CREDITS

Nick Bosanquet
Senior Research Fellow, Centre for Health Economics, University of York

The service credit proposal is up for debate. There may be better ways of achieving the aims. Behind the specific proposition lies a more general contention, namely that on the record of the last fifteen years much bigger changes are needed in policy approaches than seem likely. In a Discussion Paper for MIND, I have set out some of the reasons for this in detail(1). The actual record achieved over a period of time seems more relevant as a guide to what should be done in the future than vaguer intimations, which always tend to be optimistic, about what is going on at the moment.

The record is as follows:

-   The investment in hostels by local authorities had disappointing results in the 1970s. The concept of the small hostel with a homelike atmosphere as recommended in the 1971 White Paper(2) was not realised in practice. The 1971 White Paper was extremely optimistic about the potential for the hostel, but the 1980 Review(3) was quite pessimistic about what had actually been achieved.

-   The problems of staff training in the hostels remained great. Local authorities were not able to offer staff appropriate training.

- The number of adults in mental handicap hospitals was far higher than had been hoped for in 1971. Although day-to-day living conditions had improved greatly, the hospitals were still not able to offer active rehabilitation.

- The client in need of long-stay residential care has a choice of a 'hospital' place. Their characteristics can be explained only in terms of producer interest.

- The problems raised by monopoly are great where they exist in any activity. The impact of monopoly has been far greater than realised in these services.

- Ideas about the permanence of dependency and handicap have changed. The normalisation philosophy represents a much more optimistic view than was held in the 1960s and early 1970s about the potential for most handicapped people.

- The informal sector involving housing associations, and voluntary groups as well as social service and NHS staff, has developed much more than was expected in 1971(4). The 1971 White Paper does not in fact mention opportunities in ordinary housing.

Care in the Community is a radical programme which is getting a good response: but it does not go far enough in facing the underlying economic problem of the extra resources which will be required by the hospitals. Nor does it deal with the new possibilities raised by greater client ability to exercise choice and the potential for new patterns of service.

What is a possible new framework for service provision which would promote greater client choice as opposed to monopoly?

The framework I propose has three key components: sponsorship; service credits; and an independent agency for accreditation.

The proposals are based on a certain view of the responsibilities of the State. It is accepted that care for mentally handicapped people who cannot live with their families should be tax-financed, and it is also assumed that the State should set specific standards of care, although this monitoring role is confused at present by the self-interest of the public sector producers.

The main features of the first phase of the proposed scheme are as follows:

- The 15,000 long-stay hospital residents who have been assessed as being ready to move out quickly would be entitled to a service credit. This credit could be used to meet the costs of either the existing hospital bed or a place in the community. In the first year or two the availability of places would be such that most people would have to remain where they were, but over a period of time the choice would increase.

- The average service credit would be gauged by the average revenue costs of a long-stay hospital place - currently about £12,000 a year. The size of the credit would be related to dependency levels. In principle it should be possible to tailor the payment to the individual, as already happens with fostering.

- An independent agency would be set up to administer the payment of service credits and to make arrangements for the accreditation of new kinds of care. It would also set standards for the quality of care offered by these new services.

- Each mentally handicapped person would have his or her own sponsor: a relative if possible, a social worker from his home area or an independent person approved by the new agency if not. The sponsor would sign a written agreement to look after the client's interests. Sponsorship would be a further development of the role already played by some social workers, but would aim to create a more personal and permanent relationship with the mentally handicapped client.

Although it is not directed towards exactly the same end, the concept of citizen advocacy pioneered in Sweden and the United States might provide a useful model for the development of sponsorship. A citizen advocate is an unpaid volunteer who matches up with a resident in a mental handicap hospital, and represents that person's interests as if they were his or her own. There are a number of citizen advocacy projects in the United Kingdom, the largest of which, Advocacy Alliance(5), has placed advocates in three major London hospitals.

- The service credit would be notional as long as the mentally handicapped person remained in hospital but once the client

44

had secured a place in the community the credit would be claimed from the new central agency. The health district would then pay £12,000 a year to the agency (rather less in the initial period when there would be some support from central funds).

- Any accredited group, be it based in the public or the informal sector, would be able to provide places and to apply for the service credit.

- Some of the credit could be use to meet the cost of day care, recreation and education. (Part of the cost of a long-stay hospital place of course covers these kinds of activities.)

- Residents of hostels would also be entitled to a service credit, the cost of which would be met by central government. It would be equal to the average cost of a hostel place and would again be notional as long as the person concerned was still living in the hostel. If he secured a place elsewhere he could then claim the credit from the central agency.

- Mentally handicapped people living in the community who were assessed as being in need of supported residential care would be entitled to a service credit equal to the average cost of a long-stay hospital place. The assessment would be carried out in the normal way by health and social services with some guidelines from the new agency.

- It might well be necessary to limit the total number of credits available in order to avoid the creation of a disincentive to continued provision in the informal sector.

- Service credits would be financed mainly by redirecting the money currently used to fund hospital places, but there would be some net increase in public spending: in the shorter term a bridging element would be required. If 10,000 more places were provided in the community over a five-year period and 75 per cent of these were self-financing, the net increase in public spending would be in the order of £30 million a year.

In due course the scheme could be made available to all long-stay hospital residents; the reasons why this would not happen initially are purely pragmatic.

A service credit scheme as proposed has much to recommend it. For example, it would make tax finance available to fund a wider range of care provided by a wider range of groups. The informal sector already offers a fair amount of scope in terms of the care it provides for less severely handicapped people. There is no reason why it should not become much easier for voluntary organisations and groups of relatives to provide care for more severely handicapped people.

The proposals are based on the principle that the funding body and the body which provides the care should not be one and the same. They make it possible for a much wider range of groups and organisations to provide care, and they also aim to tilt the balance of power towards mentally handicapped people and their families. Mentally handicapped people and their sponsors would have much more influence on the kind of places provided, both through the initial specification and subsequently through their power to take their credit elsewhere.

Finally, the proposed scheme is intended to make it easier for people to move out of hospital, and the reduction in the number of long-stay places needed would provide the additional money required during the bridging period. In the long run places in hospitals and hostels would remain available only if clients and their sponsors were willing to spend their service credits on such places.

The role of the independent agency is central to the success of the proposed scheme. It is envisaged that the agency would have a staff and board of management principally comprising people of independent standing, some of them from outside the mental handicap field. It would set standards for all placements, and would carry out inspections of public and private sector provision. It would also organise the training of care staff, perhaps through a levy on projects participating in the scheme. Many kinds of voluntary groups could apply to the agency for accreditation, and accredited groups who could attract commitments in terms of service credits would then have a secure source of funding. The evidence from the group home movement suggests that there would be a strong response to secure and realistic funding.

In the future there is no reason why the service credit principle should not be applied to day care.

It should be stressed that the standards for accreditation would be stringent and that it would be far from easy to obtain. This would not be social security-led diversification. In the early stages the DHSS should shift the focus of support from the project to the organisation. Before the service credit principle could work well, there would have to be a range of providers with the confidence and ability to deliver services. The competition would come about partly through the expansion of existing voluntary organisations. There could also be new kinds of consortia bidding to provide services in an area. These might include people currently working in the official services but with different ideas from them.

There is also an important local planning job to be done. Projects cannot stand on their own but should form a network available to clients. The emphasis should be on local rather than central planning. Finally, there must be scope for much more use of fostering and of adult care schemes. At present the NHS cannot make placements directly. People who wish to undertake care on an individual basis should be able to apply for service credits.

References
1. N. Bosanquet, <u>Extending Choice for Mentally Handicapped People</u>, MIND Discussion Paper No.1, 1984.
2. Department of Health and Social Security, <u>Better Services for the Mentally Handicapped</u>, HMSO, 1971, Cmnd 4683.
3. Department of Health and Social Security, <u>Mental handicap: progress, problems and priorities, a review of mental handicap services in England since the 1971 White Paper</u>, DHSS, 1980.
4. J. Ritchie, J. Keegan and N. Bosanquet, <u>Housing for Mentally Ill and Mentally Handicapped People</u>, HMSO, 1983.
5. Headquarters at 115 Golden Lane, London EC1Y 0TJ.

TOWARDS JOINT TEAMS WITH JOINT BUDGETS? THE CASE OF THE ALL WALES STRATEGY

Gordon Grant
Mental Handicap Project, Department of Social Theory and Institutions, University of North Wales, Bangor.

This paper introduces a particular approach to joint working at the local level between health and social service workers. It raises questions to do with the accessibility and control of resources by front-line workers and families. By drawing upon the experience of one of the experimental areas in the All Wales Strategy, some contrasting perspectives are presented about the scope for fuller budgetary control by professional workers. The problems and possibilities involved rest, it is suggested, on the purpose of multi-disciplinary teamwork and inter-organisational relations in the health and social services. The paper begins with a description of the All Wales Strategy and the approach it advocates to planning and management of services.

Background

The All Wales Strategy for the Development of Services for Mentally Handicapped People(1) is the latest in a series of central government initiatives intended to stimulate the growth of local services for mentally handicapped people which are accessible, comprehensive, and integrated. In so doing, the AWS aspires to make it possible for mentally handicapped people (i) to have the right to normal patterns of life within the community,(ii) to be treated as individuals, and (iii) to expect additional help from the communities in which they live and from professional services if they are to develop their maximum potential as individuals.

In financing the strategy by direct grant aid, the Welsh Office is committing substantial sums of money accumulating to £26 million per annum by the tenth year. These monies are additional both to planned expenditure by local and health authorities and to joint finance and care in the community allocations for Wales. The greater part of the additional expenditure is planned for the second half of the ten-year period. Growth in total expenditure on mental handicap services due to the AWS amounts to about 5 per cent per annum compound in years 1-5 and about 7 per cent thereafter. The strategy is therefore releasing a significant amount of new money at a time when investment in related health and social services seems bound to remain at a standstill.

Unlike the joint financing arrangements, the funding of AWS developments does not rest on a tripartite system between central and local government and health authorities with agreed tapering mechanisms to guide the assumption of responsibilities. Nor does it depend on cash transfer linked to the discharge of residents from hospital to local authority care.

Instead, projects are directly funded by the Welsh Office and involve no immediate financial commitment from local agencies. The resources are intended to permit the gradual development of local community-based services and thereby intensify support to the 96 per cent of mentally handicapped people in Wales who live in the community in forms of accommodation other than hospital. The emphasis is on building up the existing stock of community provision rather than on the immediate run-down and closure of long-stay hospitals. Agencies in Wales have been preparing three and ten-year plans for the new services in the knowledge that there are agreed amounts of cash on the table for successive years. By generating clear financial targets for agencies for the first ten years, the AWS differs from joint finance strategies whose financial parameters change from year to year. Although therefore the AWS is free from many constraints felt to limit more effective implementation of joint finance policies(2), proposals have to be seen to be the product of a consultative process which requires statutory and voluntary bodies, and representatives of mentally handicapped people and their families, to be involved in the planning and management of services.

Towards involvement in planning and management of services
No single blueprint for the planning and management of services is advocated in the AWS but lead responsibility is expected to be taken by social services authorities for the preparation and

submission of plans and the co-ordination of management arrangements:

> given that the development of the new services will be the responsibility primarily of social services authorities, those authorities should take the lead in the preparation and submission to the Welsh Office of plans for the introduction of comprehensive services in accordance with the strategy. In doing so they must consult fully the health authority, their matching education authority, housing authorities, voluntary bodies and other relevant service providers and consumers to ensure that their necessary contribution to the support and development of services will be forthcoming. The outcome of these consultations should be recorded in the submitted plans, but this will not comprise or dilute the responsibility of individual service providing agencies for their own services.
>
> (AWS, para. 6.3.4.(i)).

> in particular formal and informal arrangements must be made to involve the representatives of mentally handicapped people and their families in the planning and management of services. It is acknowledged that there can be difficulties in finding fair and accepted procedures, especially as regards to the means of determining who shall represent consumers. For this reason no one method is insisted upon. This will have to be determined locally. Nevertheless, the local authorities will need to demonstrate to the Welsh Office that they have developed such arrangements in consultation with consumers' representatives.
>
> (AWS, para. 6.3.4.(i)).

Whilst promoting a participative approach to planning and management which requires some degree of lateral integration between agencies, the AWS also requires evidence from agencies that they have taken steps to involve consumers and their representatives in this process. At the time of writing several counties in Wales are still waiting for their plans to be accepted by the Welsh Office and this in large measure appears to be due to difficulties in providing for participation in multi-organisational planning and management contexts. Although these difficulties are acknowledged in the AWS itself, no easy solutions are perceived and much appears to rest on what might be termed local creativity, entrepreneurial skills and conceptual helmsmanship.

(i) <u>Local activity</u> The AWS appears to pin many of its hopes on the involvement of local caring agents, notably voluntary organisations, volunteers and families themselves, in the planning and management of services. The strategy refers to the 'notable record of innovation' of the voluntary sector in Wales and clearly the involvement of this source of social care in the new arrangements is seen as a route to unlocking creative potential. Similarly, the involvement of consumers and their representatives in the planning and management process is perceived as perhaps the most obvious route to acknowledging consumer needs. However, this requires a fundamental redefinition of lines of accountability and control.

(ii) <u>Entrepreneurial skills</u> An emphasis on the fashioning of new partnerships between statutory, voluntary and informal care agents provides a formidable test of the entrepreneurial capacity of people charged with managerial responsibility. So far the principle of inter-agency planning and co-ordinated management appears to have been accepted throughout most of Wales but its implementation is proving extremely difficult. Agencies and groups entering this arena have soon discovered that the balance of power between them is most unequal. This seems unlikely to change as long as any one agency is mandated to take 'lead responsibility' for planning and co-ordinated management. The requirement to adopt an underlying consultative approach in this process has the ring of participatory democracy about it, but imbalances in the knowledge, skill and conferred power between participating groups make democracy hard to realise in the inter-organisational context.

For managers at all levels, this rather uncertain and unsettling task environment creates pressures of its own. Having to plan, consult, bargain, negotiate, solve problems, review and take executive action with other agencies, and with consumers and their representatives, after a process of full and adequate consultation, means for most managers the need to learn new behaviours and new skills(3). Some three years after the launch of the AWS, it is still not inappropriate to ask how this new knowledge is to be acquired. Part of the answer lies in learning by doing. For the rest, agencies perhaps need to look beyond Wales and to the experience of joint finance and inner city partnerships in particular.

(iii) <u>Conceptual helmsmanship</u>. It is also evident that the conceptual clarity of plans submitted to the Welsh Office is highly variable between county authorities. Although there remain disputes about whether particular bodies have been consulted fully or adequately, the forms or levels of integration of planning and management between agencies are still open to debate. In short, models of pluralist enterprise are proving elusive as templates for action. Some agencies appear to want to retain their autonomy whereas others strain somewhere between what Warren terms federative and coalitional models(4), the difference between these being expressed in terms of degrees of formal collaboration for the achievement of inclusive goals between agencies. Achieving a co-ordinated inter-organisational system of planning and management without stifling the voice of consumers, their representatives and front-line service providers presents a further set of challenges to those placing a primacy, as the AWS suggests, on decentralised organisational models.

Hence, in encouraging a participative approach to planning and the fashioning of a co-ordinated management system which leads to local, accessible, integrated and comprehensive services, overarching organisational problems have to be overcome. The AWS is, however, rather more explicit about some of the irreducible ingredients of a planning and service delivery system at the local (or district) level.

Joint teams at the local level
Although again the AWS does not lay down a single blueprint for the planning, management and delivery of services at the local level, it outlines features deemed to be relevant which will need to be adapted to local circumstances as appropriate. These include the development of community mental handicap teams (CMHTs), district co-ordinators, key worker approaches, individual programme plans, a professional support system and clear operational policies. In trying to guide agencies to make balanced decisions about where decision-making responsibility should lie, the strategy makes two other general recommendations:

the importance of the full involvement and cooperation of the mentally handicapped person and his family in the preparation, implementation and monitoring of individual plans cannot be overstated. Plans must not at any stage be the product of professional assessment alone.

(AWS, para. 6.4.4.(iii)).

52

decision-making should be delegated to the lowest possible levels of staff given the opportunity to take initiatives and calculated risks so as to develop the independence and skills of those in their care.

For implementation in the intended way at the local level, the strategy appears to rely on a joint approach between CMHTs and families in the development of individual plans. It also suggests a decentralised system of management to free staff to take initiatives, something which conventional social services teams are reported to aspire to but rarely achieve(5). The AWS acknowledges that CMHTs will not themselves guarantee that services will be comprehensive nor that individuals will receive customised services. It does, however, suggest that these teams are an important pre-requisite for these developments and particularly in the way they should promote the integration of services. In the end, therefore, the success of the decentralised and participative approach advocated may well depend on sensitivity and support by the rest of the system to what CMHTs are saying.

Herein lies a major challenge, for a grass-roots participative approach can, cynically, be equated all too readily with notions of 'tail wagging dog'. The shift strongly implied by the strategy towards greater power-sharing is proving to be exceedingly threatening to agencies charged with major responsibilities for co-ordination and planning. Ironically this has already turned out to be a central and contentious issue in the two Vanguard authorities of Mid-Glamorgan and Gwynedd, whose experimental areas are to receive services at an accelerated rate and whose actions are supposed to be seen as a testing ground for the rest of Wales. Hence whilst debate and argument continue, considerable organisational inertia may remain. If the present reluctance to sacrifice some organisational autonomy and control persists much longer, willing or potential partners from the ranks of families, voluntary organisations and other agencies may well be lost to the unfolding drama. Some, sadly, have already left the stage in frustration and despair and are unlikely to return.

In talking to families as part of our research into the implementation of the AWS in the North Wales Vanguard area(6) it is quite clear that families have very varied motives for participating or not participating in the planning or delivery of services for mentally handicapped people. Although it is premature to present the full results of fieldwork which is still proceeding, it is becoming clear that some factors related to participation are recurring in interviews with a regularity that cannot be overlooked.

Firstly, families welcome the idea of a consultative approach which involves talking to families in their own homes and communities, providing a context for more private discussion. Secondly, continued participation in a planning system appears to be conditioned by the ability to turn plans into practical services. If relevant services do not materialise quickly enough, families not surprisingly begin to disengage themselves from planning systems no matter how democratic these may be. Thirdly, consultative approaches which smack of tokenism enrage some families and so make it more difficult for them to participate on a reasoned level or cause people to become disillusioned and withdraw.

Participation is also perceived by families on different levels. Almost all would wish to see the adoption of the individual programme plan type of approach at the case level. For many, especially older families, this is the only way they are likely to participate. With a substantial number of families, some control over the shaping of plans for the communities or districts in whch they live is an accompanying desire which extends therefore to concerns beyond their own mentally handicapped dependant. Finally, for what appears to be only a small number of families, participation in county-wide forums to deal with questions about overall strategy or policy is yet another important point of entry. At whatever level families engage the system in this collective enterprise, the key factor underpinning continued participation is very much tied up with questions about influence and control.

Joint teams with joint budgets?
In trying to develop responses to the varied levels on which families wish to participate in the planning process, agencies in Wales have tended to develop multi-disciplinary district and county level planning and development groups. As plans become formally adopted these groups are becoming more involved in questions about the monitoring and review of services. At the same time, increasing attention is being focussed on CMHTs as a primary point of contact with services for families.

These multi-disciplinary teams are seen as having a variety of functions which embrace the following:

-       support and advice to parents,
-       preparation and rolling forward of individual programme plans,

- mobilisation of community resources,
- facilitating contacts between consumers and voluntary bodies,
- provision of practical advice to parents and care staff,
- advocacy,
- provision of a central point of contact and information,
- provision of data about local service deficiencies,
- participation in planning of local services.

To carry out these functions effectively, CMHTs appear to require clear operational guidelines, an agreed charter between participating agencies about the purposes of multi-disciplinary teamwork, and delegated authority to implement these varied tasks. We wait to see whether these conditions can be fashioned. To concentrate on just one of the contentious issues raised by this underlying approach, the consultative process has highlighted the critical role of CMHTs in turning individual programme plans and district-based plans into practical reality and how far delegated team budgets for community care can facilitate this transition. Although the idea of bringing professional discretion and budgetary control into new unifying roles is not new(7), community care budgets for multi-disciplinary CMHTs are generating some interesting debates. From discussions with families, professionals and administrators in the North Wales Vanguard area, pro and anti-lobbies can be discerned.

Those advocating this type of budgetary control by teams talk about the need to make resource decisions on the basis of individual needs rather than by agency Diktat. They argue that CMHTs, as front-line service providers who are in regular contact with families, are therefore in the best position to make decisions about transfer of cash into service. The reasoning stems from assumptions about the need to find customised solutions to individual and local need. The AWS stresses the need for alternatives to conventional day and residential services and advocates the scaling down and de-segregation of services, something which CMHTs are uniquely placed to carry out on the basis of individual programme plans.

It is also argued that budgetary control by teams would allow greater speed and flexibility of response to individual need. Within the multi-disciplinary setting it is claimed that this would reinforce the accountability of team members to each other and provide an incentive for the setting of team priorities, and the development of teamwork itself. Since it places critical decision-making about resources closer to families, in principle it makes it more possible for them to exert some influence and control over the planning and management system and over the services they require. In this sense it makes more possible the negotiation of responsibility between informal care, voluntary and statutory organisations for support to individual clients. For the front-line workers involved it provides an incentive to pursue community mobilisation goals and to risk new behaviour within agreed parameters. If these goals can be achieved the approach may prove to be a key source of job satisfaction.

In bringing needs assessment, budgetary control and planning within the ambit of locally based teams it seems reasonable to assume that there is a chance to move away from incremental approaches which often result in maintenance of the status quo or in the foisting of new and unwanted services on front-line workers and families. Instead it places much greater responsibility for planning on their shoulders.

Whilst some workers and families in the North Wales Vanguard area have been articulating these concerns for some time, there is a strong and discernible anti-lobby. Much of this is related, predictably, to fears about the loss of agency control which was mentioned earlier. There are also risks that devolving substantial budgets to local teams will create uncontrollable precedents about the allocation of resources. Some workers, perhaps sceptical or self-effacing of their own abilities, have expressed doubts about handling the extra responsibilities involved. Certainly the integration of planning, service provision and budget control into the brief for teams is generating hitherto untested challenges. Some observers have suggested that this will only allow dominant professional groups to dictate the pattern of local service development. Others point out that it will cause too great a change to the present system of representative democracy where decisions about resources and resourcing are made by elected members. Hence a move in this direction means a re-ordering of officer-member role relationships.

Although it is acknowledged that team budgets would have to be administered through one agency, probably the Social Services Department, it appears to some unpalatable that workers employed by other agencies in the CMHT should have shared control over disbursement of community care budgets. They draw attention to the attendant need to tighten the system of accountability and control, with the risks this might create in cramping professional endeavour. Paradoxically there is then a view that creating a system for managing multi-disciplinary team budgets might undermine the very purposes that these budgets are supposed to serve.

In short, the anti-lobby is wary of the move towards greater decentralisation and mistrustful of the inter-professional and inter-organisational relations. This reluctance appears to be rooted not only in the principles concerned but in the history of intra- and inter-organisational relations within the health and personal social services.

A cautionary tale

In drawing up their county plans, most of the lead authorities in Wales have taken steps to establish locally based planning groups or work-groups within each district. This has been seen as the most obvious way of allowing ideas to filter through from the grassroots, and a means by which consumers and their representatives can involve themselves. It was through this mechanism that proposals about flexi-care budgets began to arise in the North Wales Vanguard area. These budgets were intended to give CMHTs scope to provide a service more customised to local need in just the manner outlined earlier. Explaining why this proposal has not yet become a reality involves a short cautionary tale.

To say that the idea did not receive the rubber-stamp of the central co-ordinating committee charged with final responsibility for the county plan is to oversimplify a complex tension which now exists between those working at the grassroots and those at the administrative centre. The proposal was omitted from the final plan but this was done without explanation to those suggesting it. Given the primacy attached to consultation which is supposed to underpin the planning process in the AWS, it is understandable that proposers of the idea should feel perplexed, unfairly treated and mistrusted. The rationale or assumptions of those at the centre still remain unshared with those working at the grassroots on this issue. Hence, what started out as a simple, if radical, budgetary convention has become entangled in a web of issues about the meaning of participation in the planning process and about power relations in a multi-group, multi-organisational system. It is also beginning to dawn on new entrants to this system, notably consumers and their representatives, and voluntary groups, that bureaucratic agencies do not at times behave rationally or democratically. Almost inadvertently, it seems that the groups most concerned here have stumbled over an idea which has acted as a trigger mechanism for a range of issues about which there is still considerable ambivalence. The future of decentralised approaches to budgeting may therefore depend on progress in clarifying the rather uncertain task environment of inter-organisational relations in the health and personal social services.

Discussion: towards better inter-organisational relations?

Although, in the wake of debates about the mixed economy of welfare, policy prescriptions have repeatedly drawn attention to the need for co-ordination and collaboration between agencies, and for an emphasis on the development of voluntary-statutory sector partnerships, tried and tested models are proving elusive, or so it would seem. It is also becoming clear that collaborative arrangements can serve a number of diverse, not to say conflicting, aims; for example, to reduce areas of overlap and confusion between the responsibilities of different agencies, i.e. to optimise the functional autonomy of the agencies involved; on the other hand, collaboration might mean the fostering of interdependence between agencies in order to launch new programmes which require the resources of more than one agency. Reid provides a salutary commentary on this issue(8).

In defence of agencies struggling to find routes to productive participation in a collectivist system, the whole sphere of inter-organisational relations is one which, with one or two notable exceptions, has been starved of empirical research and of model building. Although this is now being put right, there has not been the tradition of research or analysis which in the USA has led to the advancement of inter-organisation theory. Much could be gained from closer study of this literature and experience.

Hage's interesting empirical studies of mental handicap demonstration projects(9), for example, suggest the need to pose quite basic questions about inter-organisational relationships. What conceptions do the key social groups have of organisational integration or independence? How central are the aims of particular agencies to the aims of integration? How are the trade-offs between autonomy and interdependence perceived? What are the unintended consequences of integration for the agencies involved? In his own studies, Hage noted that organisations tended to avoid integration except in relatively safe areas auxiliary to the main organisational objectives.

He concludes that options such as complete mergers on the creation of centralist boards with dictatorial control would not be viable and suggests, rather, that coalitions and coalitional funding would be the preferred route to the co-ordination of complex service delivery needs. Organisations lose some autonomy but gain more power in obtaining resources from the environment. In Hage's view, where complex client needs require a delivery system of organisations, coalitions between organisations become both a functional necessity and a technological imperative. Beyond these pragmatic considerations, it is desirable to bring together three values that often conflict yet which are desirable to have represented: efficiency, quality of care and consumer need.

If Hage is right, the dialectical interplay between these interests will shape styles of multi-disciplinary teamwork and budget control. Bringing these interests together at the level of CMHTs brings the whole sphere of professional and administrative decision-making, inter-agency co-ordination and consumer involvement much more into the open. By increasing the visibility of decision-making and budget allocation relative to individual client and family needs, one is providing for a much more finely tuned self-monitoring system which may help to allay fears about letting accountability go out of the window. Devolution of authority would clearly have to be accompanied by a parallel devolution of responsibility to teams in this situation. Perhaps the most immediate questions one is left to ponder are those relating to the capacity of teams to accommodate the diverse skills and technologies involved in (i) developing methods of multi-disciplinary teamwork, (ii) budget allocation and budget control for community care needs, (iii) determining local priorities for teamwork and team-building in conjunction with consumer interests and needs and the voluntary sector, (iv) planning and review activity, and (v) casework. This represents a considerable agenda for any team of people anywhere let alone CMHTs which are still comparative fledglings in the teamwork business.

Hall and Clark's studies of inter-organisational relationships among child welfare agencies demonstrate that communication patterns could be of good quality and be used frequently but based around conflict situations(10). Contact was not necessarily a sign of consensus. The AWS experience certainly bears this out. Consultation, as the keynote to any form of joint activity, has singularly failed to establish a ready consensus. On the other hand, conflict should not necessarily be taken as a sign of system failure. It may be nothing less than the necessary clash of opinion before the burgeoning of a new idea. Hence IPP and key worker systems which provide a mechanism for drawing consumers and their representatives into a dialogue with groups like CMHTs may bring occasional if necessary discomfort to the key parties involved. There should be no pretence that it will prove to be a cosy arrangement.

Hall and Clark's work also shows that co-ordination of effort between agencies was strongly associated with factors like the importance of contacts, compatible organisational philosophies, the assessment of good performance by other agencies, and the assessment that other agencies have competent personnel. If this experience is translatable to the activities of CMHTs, we are likely to find that, even within teams, styles of teamwork and methods of linkage between individuals do no more than reflect the outcome of peer review and the process of self-monitoring by teams. This may be no bad thing if it helps team members to identify their individual and collective strengths and break through past preoccupations with professional boundaries and individualised methods of work.

The work of Marrett(11) and Van de Ven, Emmett and Koenig (12) provides useful theoretical frameworks for understanding inter-organisational relations; the former for the useful distinction between comparative and relational properties of organisations in interacting networks, and the latter for what is probably the most advanced theoretical discussion yet reported in the literature. Both these contributions provide hints about functional problems that organisational networks have to survive, if they are to survive as more or less integrated social systems. CMHTs or other multi-disciplinary groups may benefit from reflecting on these structural maintenance properties.

As Hage has observed, the interdependence usually sought in these situations requires more than the exchange of clients and information, but less than a merger or some system of hierarchical control. What appears to be sought is more than a confederation and less than a federation, and an approach which is something between an elitist and a pluralist structure. These, like other major value questions, involve a delicate balancing act and it is hardly surprising that agencies are facing obstacles which impede innovation and change. The budgetary question is central to this entire analysis. Placing highly trained groups of professionals into front-line positions such as multi-disciplinary CMHTs is an expensive business, and all the more so, it seems to the present writer, if those who counsel, support and negotiate with families have to wait for administrators and local politicians to make 'informed' decisions about releasing resources for the meeting of individual consumer need. It seems a fair bet that Hage's three criteria of efficiency, quality of care and meeting of consumer need would more easily be achieved through joint teams like CMHTs with their own community care budgets. CMHTs, however, are not autonomous units and the decision about this type of policy is likely to be taken elsewhere. As long as local budgetary priorities are determined outside the province of local CMHTs, it seems likely that the performance of teams will be determined for them rather than by them. If this continues to be the case, we seem to face a major disjunction between what statutory bodies as opposed to families want.

With ideological, organisational and budget reforms such as those advocated in the AWS, there is always a danger that they become an end in themselves rather than a means to agreed need-based ends. In the last analysis, whatever grand strategies and tactical manoeuvring organisations adopt, these need to be measured against the degree to which they help mentally handicapped people to be treated as individuals, to have the right to ordinary patterns of life, and, where necessary, to expect additional help from communities in which they live and from professionals to develop their maximum potential as individuals.

References

1. Welsh Office, All Wales Strategy for the Development of Services for Mentally Handicapped People. March, 1983.
2. National Association of Health Authorities, Mentally Ill and Mentally Handicapped People: NAHA's Position on Community Care. July, 1984.
3. Grant, G., Towards Participation in the All Wales Strategy: Issues and Processes, Mental Handicap, 13, 2,1985 pp 51-54.
3. Douglas, T., 'Change: the Implementation of the All Wales Strategy', Mental Handicap, 13, 1, 1985 pp. 14-16
4. Warren, R., 'The Interorganisational Field as a Focus for Investigation', Administrative Science Quarterly, December, 1967, pp. 396-419.
5. Stevenson, O. and Parsloe, P., Social Services Teams: the Practitioners' View. HMSO, 1978.
6. This research is supported by DHSS funds and is being carried out by Dr Stuart Humphreys and Dr Morag McGrath.
7. Challis, D. and Davies, B., 'A New Approach to Community Care for the Elderly', British Journal of Social Work, 10, 1,1980 pp. 1-18.
8. Reid, W., 'Inter-organisational Coordination in Social Welfare: a Theoretical Approach to Analysis and Intervention' in Kramer, R. and Specht, H., Readings in Community Organisation Practice. Prentice Hall, 1969, pp. 176-88.
9. Hage, J., 'A Strategy for Creating Interdependent Delivery Systems to Meet Complex Needs' in Negandhi, A., Interorganisation Theory, Kent State University Press, 1980, pp. 210-34.

10. Hall, R. and Clark, R., 'Problems in the Study of Interorganisational Relationships' in Negandhi, op.cit. pp. 111-27.
11. Marrett, C. 'On the Specification of Interorganisational Dimensions', Sociology and Social Research, 61, 1971, pp. 83-99.
12. Van de Ven, A., Emmett, D. and Koenig, R., 'Frameworks for Interorganisational Analysis', in Negandhi, op.cit. pp. 19-38.

JOINT PLANNING – THE LAST CHANCE?

Peter Westland
Under Secretary (Social Services) Association of Metropolitan Authorities

This seminar was reluctant to search for, much less identify, the necessary elements of a successful joint planning system in the pursuit of an effective community care policy. There was agreement that community care needed to be rescued from the warm glow of approbation which seems to surround the concept but obscure the often poor performance of health and local authorities. There were prescriptions about the need for more money, about the need to meet consumer demands, about the prospect of regarding social services as residual providers, about voluntary organisations as partners in the enterprise. But the submerged feeling underlying the discussions was an unspoken nostalgia for the days when optimism was fashionable; when economic growth (and incremental shares in it for the caring services) seemed possible; when planners (corporate/physical and financial) held the keys of the kingdom. In Wales, of course, with impressive and implementable plans for mentally handicapped people, they still do, but they also have continued to have real and significant growth in resources to fuel their ideas and ward off the depression which seems to have crept over planning in England.

There has, of course, been progress in the struggle towards a common description and understanding of community care amongst health and social service planners which has been increasingly supported by non-governmental organisations as providers of services. There are still some hostile professional and union forces, however, which see these concepts as a threat to power structures and to jobs, and they are sometimes held up as reasons for lack of progress. They are nothing of the sort. There is still a lack of agreement about joint planning, its purpose, its nature, and of the environment necessary for it to flourish. Of course, an atmosphere of mistrust, a belief that the Government's motivation in pressing for closure of hospitals is economic rather than therapeutic, does little to facilitate real co-operation. The Government for its part remains unconvinced that any extra money is required, even as bridging finance, for community care to progress, whilst, at the same time, local and health authorities believe equally firmly that large additional short-term funding is required if any significant programme is to be mounted at all. Otherwise, they say, community care is a diversion - something to keep the radicals out of mischief whilst the real battles are fought elsewhere.

In this climate it is not surprising that participants in the seminar looked back to the 1960s and early 1970s, when planning had a harder and more confident edge. But joint planning nowadays means sharing in development; it does not mean long-range planning, East European style, except, of course, where a hospital closure provides the driving force. Sharing in development is a softer concept but it requires either a large element of reciprocity (all parties have to show a gain of some kind if motivation is to remain high) or a new kind of altruism - something which does not usually characterise relationships between organisations. An alternative to reciprocity or altruism is, of course, central direction - that someone should tell the participants what their role should be, should limit their discretion, determine the nature and purpose of their input and the amount of money available to them.

The health service is familiar with this centralisation of power but local authorities are still fighting off the dirigiste tendencies of governments. Of course, such centralisation would lead to robotisation of planning and planners. Central regulation seemed to be favoured by the bureaucrats at the seminar but wholly rejected by the activists. The activists, or perhaps we should call them welfare opportunists, appeared to promote the view that it does not matter who provides just as long as it gets done. This is a seductively attractive proposition - why shouldn't the health service come out into the community and challenge the social services' assumed omniscience about a community's needs? To prevent health authorities from doing so could drive the NHS even further back into its institutional redoubts, and many think that this could only damage the NHS.

Pluralism is currently in vogue but pluralism can take many forms, and the kind which might lead health and local authorities to offer services in competition with each other is not one with which bureaucratic planners can possibly feel at home. Why shouldn't health and local authorities provide alternative forms of community care, giving the consumer real choice? There are some obvious answers to this, one of which is that the consumer has not, in the past, been regarded as being important enough to warrant such real choices. Another, the bureaucrats will rush in to tell us, is that, at times of scarce resources, and in relation to public expenditure, there cannot be unplanned provision – the risk of nugatory expenditure is the recurring nightmare of treasurers. Others might be more convinced of the planners' arguments if local government and the health service showed any sign, anywhere, of overproviding community care.

The rationalist in me suggests, of course, that there must be central guidance, control and even direction in order at least to ensure that something gets done. We have had a joint planning system since 1974 and it is necessary to question what it has achieved. We have had joint finance since 1976 and for many it seems that the flurry of activity surrounding the allocation of rather marginal sums of money has obscured the problems inherent in attempts jointly to plan anything. The reorganisation of the NHS in 1982 with the abolition of Area Health Authorities (where planning was supposed to take place) and the substitution of District Health Authorities as planning units was one indicator of a need to review the system. Another was the increasing financial restraints on local authorities being imposed by central government, which were thought, by many, to constitute a threat to the future of joint finance. Joint finance, although financially marginal, probably provided in many places, the incentive for health and local authorities to collaborate. How far were authorities able to extend this co-operation into genuine joint planning? The introduction by the DHSS of the 'Care in the Community' circular in 1983(1) brought a new element which explicitly permitted and encouraged transfer of resources from health to local authorities. How could joint planning harness this new opportunity; was it in fact being seized?

The Government was put under some pressure on these questions as the anxiety grew and lobbying increased during 1983. Local authorities were genuinely anxious about the future of joint finance and about the punitive penalty system of financial control which meant, for some authorities, that to pick up an extra £100,000 for assuming responsibility for projects hitherto jointly financed could cost them three times as much as Government penalised them for incurring additional expenditure. Local government began to think of joint finance, not as a short-term gain but as a medium-term albatross. The Association of Metropolitan Authorities was looking for contradictions in government policy and hoping to make capital out of them and here <u>was</u> a major inconsistency. The Government was attempting to promote the development of community care through joint finance but penalising local authorities for incurring additional expenditure.

There were some too who hoped to make 'joint planning' a euphemism for getting money for local government from the NHS. The National Association of Health Authorities - a body which had not hitherto adopted a high profile on social policy issues - had surveyed the state of joint planning just before 1982. They were worried that the new planning boundaries might interfere with the progress made. NAHA also had other reasons for pushing for a review; they wished to begin to occupy the same stage as the Local Authority Associations and preferably in collaboration with them. This would enhance NAHA's influence on government thinking. Perhaps too they thought that a joint review of joint planning might itself be a symbol of new possibilities for the future. The local authorities were of the opinion that an alliance with a 'respectable', ie. non-party political group, could be advantageous.

All seemed set then for a constructive review of joint planning and Ministers agreed in November 1983 to launch such a working party consisting of representatives of the Local Authority Associations and NAHA, with full DHSS participation. Terms of reference took a mere six months to negotiate, with much jockeying for items to be included or excluded. Ministers did not want to see any sticks with which they might be beaten emerge from the group. Civil Servants, as always, were obsessed with process; the local authorities put their emphasis on a full review of joint finance, and NAHA, in greeting the setting up of the working party, welcomed this 'Care in the Community enquiry'. The DHSS added that its main objective was to 'get people out of long-stay hospitals'.

I mention this background skirmishing only to underline the fact that joint collaborative efforts may be difficult because the participants have different agendas. There may be a short agenda of common elements but each will have other objectives. This is as true of joint planning as it is of a government-sponsored working party, and although the review was completed within a year some time was spent in mutual exploration of each other's folklore and true objectives as well as on such substantial evidence of the state of joint planning as could be mustered.

In the end the working party produced a report _Progress in Partnership_ which was predictably reformist rather than revolutionary; which advocated procedural changes; which called for heavyweight political and bureaucratic intervention at local level; which used to the full the opportunities within the existing legislation to establish a public accountability for joint planning; and which commended the many examples of good practice which it had discovered. It avoided the question of resourcing community care and by neat footwork it also avoided giving adequate reasons for failing to explore other options, ie. the transfer of responsibility for a client group entirely to one service (eg. mentally ill people to the NHS; mentally handicapped people to the local authorities). Civil Servants clearly felt that they could not recommend the transfer of responsibility for mentally handicapped people to local authorities, if for no other reason than that the Minister of Health had recently declared himself against it. Civil Servants also could not argue for more money for health or social services - at the least not in public, and not much in private either; it was simply an argument they could not get into. Some local authority officials, more accustomed perhaps to public disagreements with elected members and prepared therefore to take a few more risks, were less inhibited about advocating the abandonment of joint planning except where irreducibly necessary. This meant the assumption of responsibility of particular client groups by the NHS or local authorities. Alternatively, the free-for-all competitive concept mentioned earlier was floated but found little favour amongst any of the public servants.

The report was 'published' in July 1985 but, although distributed and discussed widely in local and health authority circles, it could not be commented on by Civil Servants because of a convention which made the document confidential until released by Ministers. A Government Minister belatedly gave it a public welcome when he launched it in December 1985 and opened it to public discussion.

What significance will it have? It aims to improve the present system by recommending specific formulations for Joint Care Planning Teams and for the activities of Joint Consultative Committees. It enjoins Chief Executives and District General Managers not simply to take joint planning seriously but either to take part in it themselves or to take personal responsibility for ensuring that their organisation participates. It asks DHSS Ministers to exercise one of the few joint planning powers they have by requiring Joint Consultative Committees to produce reports on their activities and achievements in respect of specified client groups. Regional Health Authorities are reminded of their influential role through the annual review of DHA's; however, the report stops short of suggesting that Regions should allocate joint finance (and other resources) to Districts according to the progress and relevance of joint planning activities. It recommends that joint finance should be used to establish specific posts for joint planning purposes. The working party took the view that failure to plan jointly 'stems in the main from the lack of any clear structure, aims or accountability for joint planning'. It sets out therefore, within the limitation of existing legislation and the conventional wisdom about public provision of services, to remedy these omissions and its prescriptions are clearly linked to and limited by the diagnosis.

The report's recommendations depend largely on the rationality and strong motivation of health and local authority personnel members and officials. It proposes an approach to joint planning which can work if rationality and motivation are there. But, if the evidence is to be believed, these attributes can overcome most of the idiosyncrasies of bureaucratic systems anyway. The report should, however, put the subject on the agenda of local and health authorities, and optimists will argue that this, in itself, will generate real advances. Members of the working party also concurred in this, but they acknowledged with reluctance that a health or local authority might prove recalcitrant (for whatever reason). In such cases they said 'where efforts at proper joint planning come to nothing, one authority, either health or social services, may have to take the lead on the overall planning, and as necessary and appropriate, on the provision of services for the client group concerned'.

This is not of course a licence to any authority to run off with the ball, much less to any which chooses capriciously not to play. It does recognise, however, that joint planning requires at least two willing parties, and that legislating for willingness is a hazardous business.

Joint planning is for optimists and for those realists who believe that a genuine pooling of resources used by both authorities for a single purpose might lead to a better use of those resources. For those who keep joint planning on the margin of their activities and of their budgets it is likely to be a time-consuming and usually frustrating activity. The working party's report might be described as joint planning's last chance. If it is taken seriously, the government might yet discover and be forced to acknowledge that there is more to community care than closing hospitals and a great deal more than simply making the best of what we've got.

1. DHSS, <u>Care in the Community</u>, LAC/83/5, 1983.
2. Gerald Wistow, 'Incentives for financing Community Care', in A. Webb and G. Wistow <u>editors</u>, <u>Planning, Need and Scarcity: Essays on the Personal Social Services</u>, Allen and Unwin, 1986.
3. <u>Progress in Partnership</u>, Report of the Working Group on Joint <u>Planning</u>, DHSS, July 1985.

 Policy Studies Institute

The **Policy Studies Institute** is Britain's largest independent research organisation undertaking studies of economic, industrial and social policy and the workings of political institutions.

The Institute is an educational charity, not run for profit, and is independent of all political pressure groups and commercial interests. It receives particular support from the Joseph Rowntree Memorial Trust.

The core of PSI's work is its wide-ranging programme of studies, organised and developed under six Research Groups responsible for a series of studies in the areas of the economy and the labour market, industrial development, politics and government, justice and social order, social policy and the quality of life.

The research methods include surveys, case studies, statistical analysis, literature and document search and discussion with practitioners and other researchers in seminars or groups.

A full list of PSI publications, and information about methods of ordering, are available from:

THE PUBLICATIONS DEPARTMENT
PSI, 100 Park Village East,
London NW1 3SR
Telephone: 01-387 2171

Copies of publications are displayed in PSI's reception at the above address, and are available for sale to individual purchasers.

SOCIAL SCIENCE LIBRARY

Manor Road Building
Manor Road
Oxford OX1 3UQ
Tel: (2)71093 (enquiries and renewals)
http://www.ssl.ox.ac.uk

This is a NORMAL LOAN item.

We will email you a reminder before this item is due.

Please see http://www.ssl.ox.ac.uk/lending.html
for details on:

- loan policies; these are also displayed on the notice boards and in our library guide.

- how to check when your books are due back.

- how to renew your books, including information on the maximum number of renewals.
  Items may be renewed if not reserved by another reader. Items must be renewed before the library closes on the due date.

- level of fines; fines are charged on overdue books.

Please note that this item may be recalled during Term.